First World War
and Army of Occupation
War Diary
France, Belgium and Germany

23 DIVISION
Divisional Troops
Divisional Signal Company
24 August 1915 - 31 October 1917

WO95/2177/4

The Naval & Military Press Ltd
www.nmarchive.com
Published in association with The National Archives

Published by

The Naval & Military Press Ltd

Unit 10 Ridgewood Industrial Park,

Uckfield, East Sussex,

TN22 5QE England

Tel: +44 (0) 1825 749494

www.naval-military-press.com

www.nmarchive.com

This diary has been reprinted in facsimile from the original. Any imperfections are inevitably reproduced and the quality may fall short of modern type and cartographic standards.

© **Crown Copyright**
Images reproduced by permission of The National Archives, London, England, 2015.

Contents

Document type	Place/Title	Date From	Date To
Heading	WO95/2177/4		
Heading	23rd Divl Signal Coy. R.E. Aug 1915-1917 Oct To Italy		
Heading	23rd Divl. Sir Coy Vol. 1 Aug 15 To Mar 19		
Heading	War Diary Of 23rd Divl. Signal Coy R.E. From August 24th 1915 To December 31st 1915 (Volume I)		
War Diary	Bordon	24/08/1915	24/08/1915
War Diary	Bramshott	24/08/1915	25/08/1915
War Diary	Bordon	26/08/1915	26/08/1915
War Diary	Southampton	24/08/1915	24/08/1915
War Diary	Havre	25/08/1915	26/08/1915
War Diary	Stomer	27/08/1915	27/08/1915
War Diary	Tilques	27/08/1915	05/09/1915
War Diary	Renescure	06/09/1915	06/09/1915
War Diary	Merris	07/09/1915	11/09/1915
War Diary	Croix Du Bac	12/09/1915	23/09/1915
War Diary	La Rolanderie	24/09/1915	27/09/1915
War Diary	Croix du Bac	28/09/1915	03/12/1915
War Diary	HQ Croix Du BAC 2. Ruemarle 3 Erquinghem 4 Rolanderie	04/12/1915	05/12/1915
War Diary	HQ. Croix Du BAC 2. Ruemarle 3. Rolanderie 4. Erquinghem	06/12/1915	10/12/1915
War Diary	Croix du Bac	11/12/1915	31/12/1915
Diagram etc	R.A. Airline. To 103, 104&103		
Diagram etc	Circuit Diagram		
Diagram etc	Circuit Diagram 23rd Divn 30. VIII. 15		
Diagram etc	Circuit Diagram 9. IX. 15 And 10.IX. 23rd Divn.		
Diagram etc	Diagram of 23rd Divn R.A. Buzzer Lines, 15.12.15		
Map	Circuit Diagram-23rd Divn. Signals Key		
Miscellaneous			
Heading	War Diary Of 23rd Divn. Signal Coy R.E. From Jan 1st 1916 To Feb 29. 1916		
War Diary	Croix du Bac	01/01/1916	23/02/1916
War Diary	Estaires	24/02/1916	25/02/1916
War Diary	Blaringhem	26/02/1916	28/02/1916
War Diary	Bruay	29/02/1916	29/02/1916
Diagram etc	3rd Corps Reserve Division Circuits 15.2.16		
Diagram etc	Circuit Diagram Estaires 25.2.16		
Heading	War Diary Of 23rd Divn. Signal Coy R.E. From Mar 1st 1916 To April 30th 1916		
War Diary	Bruay	01/03/1916	04/03/1916
War Diary	Bruay And Petit Servins	04/03/1916	04/03/1916
War Diary	Bruay & Ph. Servins	05/03/1916	07/03/1916
War Diary	Chau De La Haie & Ptt. Servins	08/03/1916	10/03/1916
War Diary	Chau De La Haie	11/03/1916	15/03/1916
War Diary	Bruay	16/03/1916	21/03/1916
War Diary	Sains-en-Gohelle	22/03/1916	18/04/1916
War Diary	Bruay	19/04/1916	30/04/1916
Diagram etc	Circuit Diagram 23rd Div. 29.2.16		
Diagram etc	Circuit Diagram. 12.3.16		

Diagram etc	Diagram of Lines 23rd Division.		
Diagram etc	Circuit Diagram 17.3.16		
Diagram etc	Y W Circuit Diagram 18/4/16		
Map	Scheme Of Divisional Lines 18.4.16		
Map	Scheme Of Brigade Lines 18-4-16		
Heading	War Diary Of 23rd Divl. Signal Coy R.E. For May 1916		
War Diary	Bruay	01/05/1916	12/05/1916
War Diary	Sains En Gohelle	13/05/1916	31/05/1916
Diagram etc	Y W Circuit Diagram 10-6-16		
Map			
Map	Training Showing Divisional Telephone		
Map	Scheme Of Brigade Lines		
Heading	Signal Coy 23rd Vol 6.7		
Heading	War Diary Of 23rd Divl. Signal Coy R.E. For June 1916		
War Diary	Sains-en-Gohelle	01/06/1916	13/06/1916
War Diary	Bruay	14/06/1916	15/06/1916
War Diary	Bomy	16/06/1916	24/06/1916
War Diary	Vaux	25/06/1916	30/06/1916
Miscellaneous	Subsidiary Means Of Signalling.	14/06/1916	14/06/1916
Diagram etc	Circuit Diagram 26.6.16		
Diagram etc	YW Circuit Diagram 14th June 1916		
Map	Ra Lines In Souchez Section 12.6.16		
Diagram etc	Training Swing Divisional Telephone.		
Map	Plan Shewing Routes Of Buried Cable June 1916		
Map	23rd Division Signals Scheme Of Communications. June 1916		
Diagram etc	Angres Group Brigade Lines June 1916		
Diagram etc	Scheme Of Brigade Lines		
Diagram etc	Circuit Diagram YW 14/6/16		
Diagram etc	Circuit Diagram YW Bomy 16th To 23rd June 1916		
Diagram etc	Circuit Diagram YW 30.6.16		
Heading	War Diary Of 23rd Div Signal Coy R.E. 1st-31st July 1916		
War Diary	Vaux-en-Amienois	01/07/1916	01/07/1916
War Diary	Baizieux	02/07/1916	03/07/1916
War Diary	Moulin du Vivier	04/07/1916	10/07/1916
War Diary	St Gratien	11/07/1916	20/07/1916
War Diary	Henencourt	21/07/1916	25/07/1916
War Diary	Albert	26/07/1916	31/07/1916
Diagram etc	Circuit Diagram YW 2.7.16		
War Diary	Circuit Diagram YW 5.7.16		
Diagram etc	Circuit Diagram YW Forward Lines 6.7.16		
Diagram etc	Circuit Diagram YW 26.7.16		
Diagram etc			
Heading	23rd Divisional Engineers 23rd Divisional Signal Company R.E. August 1916		
Heading	War Diary Of 23rd Signal Coy R.E. 1st-31st August 1916		
War Diary	Albert	01/08/1916	07/08/1916
War Diary	Baizieux	07/08/1916	10/08/1916
War Diary	Ailly-Le Haut Clocher	11/08/1916	12/08/1916
War Diary	Fletre	13/08/1916	16/08/1916
War Diary	Steenwerck	17/08/1916	28/08/1916
War Diary	Bailleul	29/08/1916	31/08/1916

Type	Description	From	To
Diagram etc	Circuit Diagram 23rd Divn. Baizieux Aug. 8th-11th.		
Map	Mametz Wood		
Map	YW Communications August 5th 16		
Map	Fighting Lines YW-July 10th Capture. or Contalmaison		
Diagram etc	Signals YW. Circuits-July 31st 1916		
Diagram etc	Signals YW. Circuits-Aug 6th 1916		
Heading	War Diary Of 23rd Signal Coy. R.E. 1st 30th September 1916		
War Diary	Bailleul	01/09/1916	04/09/1916
War Diary	Tilques	05/09/1916	09/09/1916
War Diary	Allonville	10/09/1916	11/09/1916
War Diary	Baizieux	12/09/1916	18/09/1916
War Diary	Mullencourt Albert Road	19/09/1916	23/09/1916
War Diary	Albert	24/09/1916	30/09/1916
Diagram etc	Circuit Diagram-Tilques 6.9.16		
Diagram etc	Circuit Diagram Baizieux 12.9.16		
Diagram etc	69th Inf Bde Diagram Of Lines Contalmaison		
Diagram etc	70th Inf. Bde. Diagram Of Lines		
Diagram etc	70th Inf Bde. Diagram Of Lines.		
Diagram etc	Diagram of Lines 70th Inf Bde.		
Diagram etc	Straight Line Diagram 23rd Sig Coy R.E. Oct. 5th 1916		
Diagram etc	Route Diagram Of Lines Of Communication 23rd Signal Coy R.E. Oct. 1st 1916		
Heading	War Diary Of 23rd Signal Coy R.E. 1st-31st October 1916		
War Diary	Shelter Wood	01/10/1916	08/10/1916
War Diary	Montigny	09/10/1916	11/10/1916
War Diary	Ailly-Le Haut-Clocher	12/10/1916	12/10/1916
War Diary	St Riquier	13/10/1916	14/10/1916
War Diary	Conteville	15/10/1916	15/10/1916
War Diary	Busseboom	16/10/1916	19/10/1916
War Diary	Reninghelst	20/10/1916	31/10/1916
Heading	Confidential War Diary Of 23rd Signal Coy R.E. 1st-30th November 1916		
War Diary	Reninghelst	01/11/1916	30/11/1916
Heading	Confidential War Diary Of 23rd Signal Coy., R.E. 1st-31st December 1916		
War Diary	Reninghelst	01/12/1916	31/12/1916
Map	Telephone Lines Angres Group		
Heading	War Diary Of 23rd Signal Coy RE 1st-31st January 1917		
War Diary	Reninghelst	01/01/1917	31/01/1917
Heading	War Diary Of 23rd Div. Signal Coy RE 1st To 28th February 1917		
War Diary	Reninghelst	01/02/1917	24/02/1917
War Diary	Likeman Capelle	25/02/1917	25/02/1917
War Diary	Arques	26/02/1917	28/02/1917
Heading	War Diary Of 23rd Div. Signal Coy RE 1st To 31st March 1917		
War Diary	Arques	01/03/1917	19/03/1917
War Diary	Esquelbecq	20/03/1917	31/03/1917
Heading	War Diary Of 23rd Div. Signal Coy RE 1st To 30th April 1917		
War Diary	Esquelbecq	01/04/1917	07/04/1917
War Diary	Busseboom	08/04/1917	30/04/1917

Heading	War Diary Of 23rd Signal Coy RE 1st To 31st May 1917		
War Diary	Busseboom	01/05/1917	01/05/1917
War Diary	Winnezeele	02/05/1917	11/05/1917
War Diary	Busseboom	12/05/1917	31/05/1917
Heading	War Diary Of 23rd Signal Coy RE 1st To 30th June 1917		
War Diary	Busseboom	01/06/1917	12/06/1917
War Diary	Berthen	13/06/1917	30/06/1917
Heading	War Diary Of 23rd Div. Signal Coy RE 1st To 31st July 1917		
War Diary	Zevecoten	01/07/1917	22/07/1917
War Diary	Meteren	23/07/1917	31/07/1917
Heading	War Diary Of 23rd Div Signal Coy RE 1st To 31st August 1917		
War Diary	Meteren	01/08/1917	06/08/1917
War Diary	Wizernes	07/08/1917	09/08/1917
War Diary	Eperlecques	10/08/1917	23/08/1917
War Diary	Noordpeene	24/08/1917	24/08/1917
War Diary	Reninghelst	25/08/1917	26/08/1917
War Diary	Dickebusch	27/08/1917	31/08/1917
Heading	War Diary Of 23rd Signal Coy RE 1st To 30th Sept. 1917 Vol 22		
War Diary	Dickebusch	01/09/1917	02/09/1917
War Diary	Steenvoorde	03/09/1917	04/09/1917
War Diary	Lederzeele	05/09/1917	13/09/1917
War Diary	Steenvorde	14/09/1917	14/09/1917
War Diary	Burgomaster	15/09/1917	25/09/1917
War Diary	Westoutre	26/09/1917	28/09/1917
War Diary	Burgomaster	29/09/1917	30/09/1917
Heading	War Diary Of 23rd Signal Coy RE 1st To 31st October 1917		
War Diary	Burgomaster Fm Dickebusch	01/10/1917	01/10/1917
War Diary	Berthen	02/10/1917	09/10/1917
War Diary	Chateau Segard	11/10/1917	22/10/1917
War Diary	Eecke	23/10/1917	23/10/1917
War Diary	Wizernes	24/10/1917	31/10/1917

WO 95/21774

23RD DIVISION

23RD DIVL SIGNAL COY. R.E.

AUG 1915 - ~~MAR 1918~~
1917 OCT

TO ITALY

23rd British Sig: Cor
Vol. I

7884/121

Aug '15
to
Nov '15

WAR DIARY
INTELLIGENCE SUMMARY

Army Form C. 2118.

CONFIDENTIAL

War Diary
of
23rd Divl. Signal Coy R.E.

from August 24th 1915
to December 31st 1915.

(Volume I)

Davies
Major R.E.
O.C. 23rd Sig Coy R.E.

3/1/16

Army Form C. 2118.

WAR DIARY
or
INTELLIGENCE SUMMARY.
(Erase heading not required.)

Instructions regarding War Diaries and Intelligence Summaries are contained in F. S. Regs., Part II. and the Staff Manual respectively. Title pages will be prepared in manuscript.

Place	Date	Hour	Summary of Events and Information	Remarks and references to Appendices
BORDON	24 Aug 1915	12.5 pm	HQ & Nº1 Section left BORDON by train for SOUTHAMPTON	
BRAMSHOTT	24 Aug 1915	11.30 am	Nº2 (Brigade) Section left LIPHOOK by train for SOUTHAMPTON	Jnl.
do	25 Aug 1915	12.30 pm	Nº3 (Brigade) Section left LIPHOOK by train for SOUTHAMPTON	
BORDON	26 Aug 1915	12.30 pm	Nº4 (Brigade) Section left BORDON by train for SOUTHAMPTON	
SOUTHAMPTON	24 Aug	5.30 pm / 7.0 pm	HQ and Nº1 Section left SOUTHAMPTON in the { S.S. ARCHIMEDES / S.S. MARGUERITE }	Jnl.
HAVRE	25 Aug	9.0 am / 6.0 am	do — disembarked at HAVRE and marched to Nº5 Camp.	Jnl.
HAVRE	26 Aug	10.39 am	do — left HAVRE by train.	Jnl.
ST OMER	27 Aug	4.30 am	do — detrained and marched to TILQUES to billets at the Proprieté d'ABRIMCOURT	Jnl.

WAR DIARY
or
INTELLIGENCE SUMMARY.
(Erase heading not required.)

Army Form C. 2118.

Place	Date	Hour	Summary of Events and Information	Remarks and references to Appendices
TILQUES	27 Aug	—	Laid the following lines:— 23 Div HQ (Propriété van TROYEM) to 23 Div Q Branch (Ch^au de HOGUET) Ditto to C.R.A. Ditto to 68th Bde HQ (HOULLE) And took over Signal Office at Ch^au de HOGUET from G.H.Q. operators.	J.W.
TILQUES	28 Aug	—	Laid the following lines:— 23 Div HQ (Propriété van TROYEM) to 69th Bde HQ (WESTROVE) Ditto to bridge at NORDAUSQUES	J.W. See Plan C
TILQUES	29 Aug	—	Shifted 23 Div HQ from Propriété van TROYEM to Ch^au de HOGUET. Laid the following lines: From bridge at NORDAUSQUES to 70th Bde HQ at NIELLES-les-Ardres. Ditto to 102nd RFA Bde at RUMIGHEM To tee in on line to C.R.A. 2 Lines from new 23 Div HQ	J.W.
TILQUES	30 Aug	—	Laid the following lines:— Rd-junction S of L in Eperlecques to 105th RFA Bde (BONNINGUES) 23 Div HQ (Ch^au de HOGUET) to G.O.C's billet (Propriété van TROYEM) To C.R.A's billet (Ch^au TALIN ARGENOT) Teed in on 102nd line at POLINCOVE for 103rd, and on 105th line at TOURNEHEM for 104th Bde.	J.W.

Army Form C. 2118.

WAR DIARY
or
INTELLIGENCE SUMMARY.
(Erase heading not required.)

Instructions regarding War Diaries and Intelligence Summaries are contained in F. S. Regs., Part II. and the Staff Manual respectively. Title pages will be prepared in manuscript.

Place	Date	Hour	Summary of Events and Information	Remarks and references to Appendices
TILQUES	31 Aug	—	Operating & Maintenance only.	Nil.
do	1 Sept	—	Operating & Maintenance only.	Nil.
do	2 Sept	—	Operating & Maintenance only.	Nil.
do	3 Sept	—	Operating & Maintenance only.	Nil.
do	4 Sept	—	Operating & Maintenance. Laid from WOLPHUS to ZOUAFQUES, to connect with D.A.C.	Nil.
do	5 Sept	—	Reeled up all lines	Nil.
RENESCURE	6 Sept	—	Marched from TILQUES via S. MARTIN and ARQUES to RENESCURE	
MERRIS	7 Sept	—	Marched from RENESCURE via HAZEBROUCK to MERRIS. Laid the following lines :— from STRAZEELE (104th Bde. R.F.A.) to MERRIS (Div HQ) from MERRIS (Div HQ) to LE VERRIER (69th Bde) from MERRIS (Div HQ) to NOOTE BOOM (68th Bde) from MERRIS (Div HQ) to OULTERSTEENE (70th Bde)	Nil.
MERRIS	8 Sept	—	Sent a party of 1 officer and 13 men to CROIX du BAC to be attached to 27th Signal Coy, R.E. for instruction. Laid the following lines :— from Petit SEC BOIS (103rd Bde R.F.A.) to Au SOUVERAIN (D.A.Column) from MERRIS (Div HQ) to Petit SEC BOIS from MERRIS (Div HQ) to VERTE RUE (102nd Bde R.F.A.) from MERRIS (Div HQ) to BORRE (105th Bde R.F.A.) from STRAZEELE (104th Bde R.F.A.)	Nil.

Army Form C. 2118.

WAR DIARY
or
INTELLIGENCE SUMMARY.
(Erase heading not required.)

Instructions regarding War Diaries and Intelligence Summaries are contained in F. S. Regs., Part II. and the Staff Manual respectively. Title pages will be prepared in manuscript.

Place	Date	Hour	Summary of Events and Information	Remarks and references to Appendices
MERRIS	9 Sept	—	Operating and Maintenance only.	Ovl. See Plan D
MERRIS	10 Sept	—	In accordance with orders to economize cable, reeled up portions of 4 lines making necessary tees. Operating and Maintenance.	Ovl
MERRIS	11 Sept	—	Reeled up all lines in the afternoon, orders to move having been received at 11.0 a.m.	Ovl
CROIX du BAC	12 Sept	—	Marched to CROIX du BAC, HQ of 27th Division; leaving motor-cyclists only to run HQ Signal Office.	Ovl
CROIX du BAC	13 Sept	—	Ordered by G.O.C. at 12 noon to arrange for our left brigade to take over 27th Division right bde HQ and our right brigade to occupy Divl Advanced Report Centre at ROLANDERIE Farm. Four bearer-parties went out with limbered-wagons at 2.30 p.m. and laid the following lines:— from new left bde HQ at RUE MARLE to tee into SR2 from new left bde HQ to CHAPELLE D'ARMENTIÈRE to tee into E2 from —— do —— to —— do —— to tee into KG and two lines from old left bde HQ at CHAPELLE D'ARMENTIÈRE to new left bde HQ at RUE MARLE. All lines through at 3.15 a.m., work delayed by shell-fire.	Ovl.
CROIX du BAC	14 Sept	—	Yesterday's lines made "safe" by 12 noon. Parties under instruction by 27th Signal Co. R.E.	Ovl.
CROIX du BAC	15 Sept	—	Parties under instruction by 27th Signal Co. R.E.	Ovl.
CROIX du BAC	16 Sept	—	At 10.0 a.m. took over from 27th Signal Co. R.E., 23rd Divl HQ arriving at that time.	Ovl.

Army Form C. 2118.

WAR DIARY
or
INTELLIGENCE SUMMARY.
(Erase heading not required.)

Instructions regarding War Diaries and Intelligence Summaries are contained in F.S. Regs., Part II and the Staff Manual respectively. Title pages will be prepared in manuscript.

Place	Date	Hour	Summary of Events and Information	Remarks and references to Appendices
CROIX DU BAC	17 Sept		Operating and Maintenance only.	M
CROIX DU BAC	18 Sept		Operating and Maintenance only.	M
CROIX DU BAC	19 Sept		Operating and Maintenance.	M
do	20 Sept		Operating and Maintenance. Buzzer class started 30 R.F.A. and Infantry.	M
do	21 Sept		Operating and Maintenance. Laid lines from Div Adv HQ to R.A. Adv Group HQ (A and B)	M
do	22 Sept		Operating and Maintenance. 2nd Lieut H.L.P.Tully R.E. 20 Signal Coy R.E. reported for duty vice Frevermark M	M
do	23 Sept		Operating and Maintenance. Laid lines from ERQUINGHEM (69° Field Ambulance) to ROLANDERIE.	M
do	24 Sept		Operating and Maintenance. Laid lines from Right Bde Adv HQ to 25th Bde Adv HQ from GRIS POT Dressing-Station to Right Bde Adv HQ.	M
LA ROLANDERIE	25 Sept		3 Officers and 36 NCOs & men moved to 23rd Division Advanced Report Centre & opened office at 4.0 pm. Laid line from ERQUINGHEM to ROLANDERIE & to 70° F.Ambulance. D/103	M
do	26 Sept		Operating and Maintenance, laid at night line from A Group Adv HQ to a battery in the Rue des CHARLES MI laid a line from ROLANDERIE to GRIS POT	See Plan "A"
do	27 Sept		Operating and Maintenance replaced a D1 line from ROLANDERIE to R-Bde Adv HQ by D5. Picked up line from GRIS POT Dressing Station to R-Bde Adv HQ + relaid from A Group Adv HQ to C/103 at GRIS POT. Divisional Advanced Report Centre closed at 5.0 pm + party returned to Divisional H.Q. Laid a line from BAC St MAUR (Tès & BSMI) to LORING'S Bde, FORT ROMPU	M
CROIX DU BAC	28 Sept		Operating and Maintenance	M

Army Form C. 2118.

WAR DIARY
or
INTELLIGENCE SUMMARY.
(Erase heading not required.)

Instructions regarding War Diaries and Intelligence Summaries are contained in F.S. Regs., Part II. and the Staff Manual respectively. Title pages will be prepared in manuscript.

Place	Date	Hour	Summary of Events and Information	Remarks and references to Appendices
CROIX du BAC	29 Sept	—	Operating and Maintenance.	JM
do	30 Sept	—	Operating and Maintenance. Laid lines from 105th Bde (RUE MARLE) to LORING'S Bde (FORT ROMPU); from 105th Bde & A/105 at GRIS POT, from 104th Bde (RUE MARLE) to B/103 (BOIS GRENIER)	JM
do	1 Oct	—	Operating and Maintenance. Laid line from RUE MARLE (105th Bde) to ROLANDERIE; connected to Teeing A Group and Loring's Bde and 105th Bde.	JM
do	2 Oct	—	Operating and Maintenance. Reeled up line from RUE MARLE (105th Bde) to ROLANDERIE	JM
do	3 Oct	—	Operating and Maintenance. Relaid nearly the whole of FR 3 and FR 3A South of ERQUINGHEM road and connected up with Rt Bde at ERQUINGHEM.	JM
do	4 Oct	—	Operating and Maintenance.	JM
do	5 Oct	—	Operating and Maintenance. Tied in to FR 1 and laid a line to O.C. 23rd Divl Reserve at FORT ROMPU	JM
do	6 Oct	—	Operating and Maintenance.	JM
do	7 Oct	—	Operating and Maintenance. Erected airline from Gr m FR 3A to ROLANDERIE to 69th FD Ambulance	JM
do	8 Oct	—	Operating and Maintenance.	JM
do	9 Oct	—	Operating and Maintenance.	JM
do	10 Oct	—	Operating and Maintenance.	JM

Army Form C. 2118.

WAR DIARY
or
INTELLIGENCE SUMMARY.
(Erase heading not required)

Instructions regarding War Diaries and Intelligence Summaries are contained in F. S. Regs., Part II. and the Staff Manual respectively. Title pages will be prepared in manuscript.

Place	Date	Hour	Summary of Events and Information	Remarks and references to Appendices
CROIX du BAC	11 Oct		Operating & Maintenance.	Pnj
Do	12 Oct		Operating & Maintenance.	Pnj
Do	13 Oct		Operating & Maintenance; reeled up cable from Divl H.Q. to old Reserve Bde H.Q. STEENWERK	Pm
Do	14 Oct		Operating & Maintenance.	Pm
Do	15 Oct		Operating & Maintenance.	am
Do	16 Oct		Operating & Maintenance; started new scheme of concentrating lines at YWR instead of at spanhout; PN1 and PN2; Joint Buzzer-Class Diamond YW by picking up A PN1 & PN2; fitted up office at STEENWERK for H.Q. 24th Bde	Pm
Do	17 Oct		Operating & Maintenance; erected aerials from YW to Divl Amm Col. (& Pt MORTIER)	am
Do	18 Oct		Operating & Maintenance; Second Buzzer-Class of 30 R.F.A. and Infantry joined D.A.C. aerials into HQ 20th A.T.C. R.E. and reeld	Pm
Do	19 Oct		Operating & Maintenance; ran a tee from D.A.C. up cable from D.A.C. to YWR.	Pm
Do	20 Oct		Operating & Maintenance	Pm
Do	21 Oct		Operating & Maintenance.	Pm
Do	22 Oct		Operating & Maintenance. Erected new line FRO from Divl HQ to R. LYS	Pm
Do	23 Oct		Operating & Maintenance. Continued FRO to fields beyond FORT ROMPU.	Pm

Army Form C. 2118.

WAR DIARY
or
INTELLIGENCE SUMMARY.
(Erase heading not required.)

Instructions regarding War Diaries and Intelligence Summaries are contained in F. S. Regs., Part II. and the Staff Manual respectively. Title pages will be prepared in manuscript.

Place	Date	Hour	Summary of Events and Information	Remarks and references to Appendices
CROIX du BAC	24 Oct		Operating & Maintenance.	?M
do	25 Oct		Operating & Maintenance. Picked up PN3 from YW to EPINETTE	?M
do	26 Oct		Operating & Maintenance. Picked up PN3 and PN4 from EPINETTE to PONT de NIEPPE.	?M
do	27 Oct		Operating & Maintenance. Picked up remainder of PN4 from EPINETTE to YW.	?M
do	28 Oct		Operating & Maintenance. Continued FR0 and FR1 from FORT ROMPU.	?M
do	29 Oct		Operating & Maintenance. Finished FR0 and FR1 into ROLANDERIE. Party lent by 3rd Corps erected 2 pairs from ERQUINGHEM to ROLANDERIE; also from Rt Bde HQ outfrom A Group HQ	?M
do	30 Oct		Operating & Maintenance. Ran a tee from 105 Bde – Envig's Bde line to YWR; put in permanent poles hit from 102 Bde to YWR. Party from 3rd Corps erected 2 pairs from R.A. metallic to YWR	?M
do	31 Oct		Operating & Maintenance. Dismantled PN5 from N. of ERQUINGHEM to R.E. Park; put in permanent poles between FR3, FR3A to YWR and from FR2 to FR4.	?M
do	1 Nov		Operating & Maintenance. 3rd Corps party erected 2 prs to YWR from FR2 to FR4. 3rd Corps party ran air line from SD Div. to ERQUINGHEM to YW now complete, and exchange	?M
do	2 Nov		Operating & Maintenance. Concentration of lines in YWR installed of YW now complete. working direct.	?M
do	3 Nov		Operating & Maintenance. About 1.30 p.m. 3 shells carried away all tee lines in one bay of permanent poles along the railway at ERQUINGHEM dead-ending, also 3 lines which crossed the railway; 4.10 A party was called for from CROIX du BAC and all Divisional lines were strung to	?M
do	4 Nov		Operating & Maintenance.	?M

Army Form C. 2118.

WAR DIARY
or
INTELLIGENCE SUMMARY.
(Erase heading not required.)

Instructions regarding War Diaries and Intelligence Summaries are contained in F.S. Regs., Part II. and the Staff Manual respectively. Title pages will be prepared in manuscript.

Place	Date	Hour	Summary of Events and Information	Remarks and references to Appendices
CROIX DU BAC	5 Nov		Working & Maintenance of Communications	2nd
Do	6 Nov		Ditto	2nd See Plan F
Do	7 Nov		Ditto	2nd
Do	8 Nov		Ditto. 3rd Buzzer-Clams started.	2nd
Do	9 Nov		Ditto	2nd
Do	10 Nov		Ditto	2nd
Do	11 Nov		Ditto	2nd
Do	12 Nov		Ditto Erected a line from 70th F.d Amb. at ERQUINGHEM to 70th F.A Dressing-Station at CHAPELLE D'ARMENTIÈRES.	2nd
Do	13 Nov		Ditto	2nd
Do	14 Nov		Ditto	2nd
Do	15 Nov		Ditto	2nd
Do	16 Nov		Ditto	2nd
Do	17 Nov		Ditto	2nd

WAR DIARY
or
INTELLIGENCE SUMMARY
(Erase heading not required.)

Army Form C. 2118.

Place	Date	Hour	Summary of Events and Information	Remarks and references to Appendices
CROIX DU BAC	18 Nov	—	Working & Maintenance of Communications. N° 64 L.m. INDORE was killed by a shell at RUE MARLE. Re-erected line to D.A.C. blown down by storm.	m
do	19 Nov	—	ditto	m
do	20 Nov	—	ditto	m
do	21 Nov	—	ditto. Started new scheme; all lines to be standardized so that similar lines exist in Right & Left Divisions and no more. Repaired 3 permanent lines from FORT ROMPU to ERQUINGHEM.	m
do	22 Nov	—	ditto. Laid 3 new lines from YWR to PA new position at ROLANDERIE.	m
do	23 Nov	—	ditto. Putting permanent lines in order in ERQUINGHEM - ARMENTIÈRES road.	m
do	24 Nov	—	ditto. Connected YW - PB by telephone-pair, permanent line from FORT ROMPU to SECHE RUE, owned by polcd cable + civic air line; took BSM 5 from YWR.	m
do	25 Nov	—	ditto. Brought into YW 3 lines handed over by 3rd Corps, FR 7, 8 + 9; crossed R. LYS at CRC on permanent poles. Installed all FR lines on poles on road at ERQUINGHEM.	m
do	26 Nov	—	ditto. Connected telephone to 21st Div from YWR; re-constructed pole at ERQUINGHEM.	m
do	27 Nov	—	ditto. Traced new line from RE Park to ARMENTIÈRES.	m
do	28 Nov	—	ditto. Put in extra FR 7-8. ERQUINGHEM to SECHE RUE; dis FR 9 ERQUINGHEM to RE Park + Sub Park replacing cable.	m
do	29 Nov	—	ditto.	m
do	30 Nov	—	ditto. 4" Tongue - Class started. All changes necessitated by Corps Order standardizing lines now complete, except R.A. changes.	m

WAR DIARY
or
INTELLIGENCE SUMMARY.
(Erase heading not required.)

Army Form C. 2118.

Instructions regarding War Diaries and Intelligence Summaries are contained in F.S. Regs., Part II. and the Staff Manual respectively. Title pages will be prepared in manuscript.

Place	Date	Hour	Summary of Events and Information	Remarks and references to Appendices
CROIX du BAC	1 Dec		Working & Maintenance of Communications. Started work in charge necessary F.R.A. lines under standardization scheme. Erected 2 lines from YWR to Railway crossing and 1 line from YWR & ERQUINGHEM HALT	nil
do	2 Dec		Ditto.	nil
do	3 Dec		Ditto. Completed line to meet R.A. of 20th Div.	nil
HQ. CROIX du BAC 2. RUEMARLE 3. ERQUINGHEM 4. ROLANDERIE	4 Dec		Ditto. Erected line to Montrin Battery	nil
	5 Dec		Ditto. Started relaying up SR1 & SR2 & replacing by airline, as part of scheme to replace all cable N. of a line ROLANDERIE – RUE MARLE by airline, under Corps orders.	nil
HQ. CROIX du BAC 2. RUEMARLE 3. ROLANDERIE 4. ERQUINGHEM	6 Dec		Ditto. Continued reeling up SR1 & SR2 & replacing by airline.	nil
Ditto	7 Dec		Ditto. Continued reeling up SR1 & SR2 & replacing by airline.	nil
Ditto	8 Dec		Ditto. Erecting airline to replace cable reeled up by Corps party.	nil
Ditto	9 Dec		Ditto. Replaced cable by airline N. of line ROLANDERIE – RUE MARLE; Corps party reeling up. Four men of N°4 Sec. unloading shell-fire at ERQUINGHEM	nil
Ditto	10 Dec		Ditto. Replaced cable by airline N. of line ROLANDERIE – RUE MARLE; Corps party reeling up.	nil

WAR DIARY
or
INTELLIGENCE SUMMARY.
(Erase heading not required.)

Army Form C. 2118.

Place	Date	Hour	Summary of Events and Information	Remarks and references to Appendices
CROIX DU BAC	11 Dec		Operating & Maintenance of Communication. Replacing Cable N. of ROLANDERIE - RUE MARLE line; Corps party reeling up.	m
do	12 Dec		Operating & Maintenance of Communication. As above	m
do	13 Dec		Operating & Maintenance of Communication. As above	m
do	14 Dec		Operating & Maintenance of Communication. No 2 & ERQUINGHEM; No 4 & RUE MARLE; replacing cable 3 airline. Corps party reeling up.	m
do	15 Dec		Operating & Maintenance of Communication. Continued replacing cable. Corps party reeling up.	m See Plan E
do	16 Dec		Operating & Maintenance of Communication. As above	m
do	17 Dec		Operating & Maintenance of Communication. As above	m
do	18 Dec		Operating & Maintenance of Communication. 4th Bugss - Claro Diminied. Corps party left. Reinstruction complete	m
do	19 Dec		Operating & Maintenance of Communication.	m
do	20 Dec		Operating & Maintenance of Communication. Started labelling all lines according to Corps Scheme.	m
do	21 Dec		Operating & Maintenance of Communication. Continued labelling.	m

Army Form C. 2118.

WAR DIARY
or
INTELLIGENCE SUMMARY.
(Erase heading not required.)

Instructions regarding War Diaries and Intelligence Summaries are contained in F. S. Regs., Part II. and the Staff Manual respectively. Title pages will be prepared in manuscript.

Place	Date	Hour	Summary of Events and Information	Remarks and references to Appendices
CROIX DU BAC	22 Dec		Operating & Maintenance. Labelling all lines in accordance with Corps Scheme. N° 2 to ROLANDERIE, N° 3 to ERQUINGHEM.	m
Do	23 Dec		Operating & Maintenance. Labelling & overhauling named cable.	m
Do	24 Dec		Operating & Maintenance. Erecting 4-line Comic from YW to BAC ST MAUR.	m
Do	25 Dec		Operating & Maintenance.	m
Do	26 Dec		Operating & Maintenance. Erecting 4-line Comic from YW to BAC ST MAUR	m
Do	27 Dec		Operating & Maintenance. as above 3 men of N° 4 Sec. wounded by shrapnel	m
Do	28 Dec		Operating & Maintenance. as above	m
Do	29 Dec		Operating & Maintenance. as above. 5.5" Bmzr - Class annulled.	m
Do	30 Dec		Operating & Maintenance. Erecting 4-line comic from YW to BAC ST MAUR. N° 3 to RUE MARLE ; N° 4 to ERQUINGHEM	m
Do	31 Dec		Operating & Maintenance. Arranging artillery communication for night-raids in both sectors.	m See Plan B

Jales, Major R.E.
O.C. 23rd Sig. Coy R.E.
3·1·16

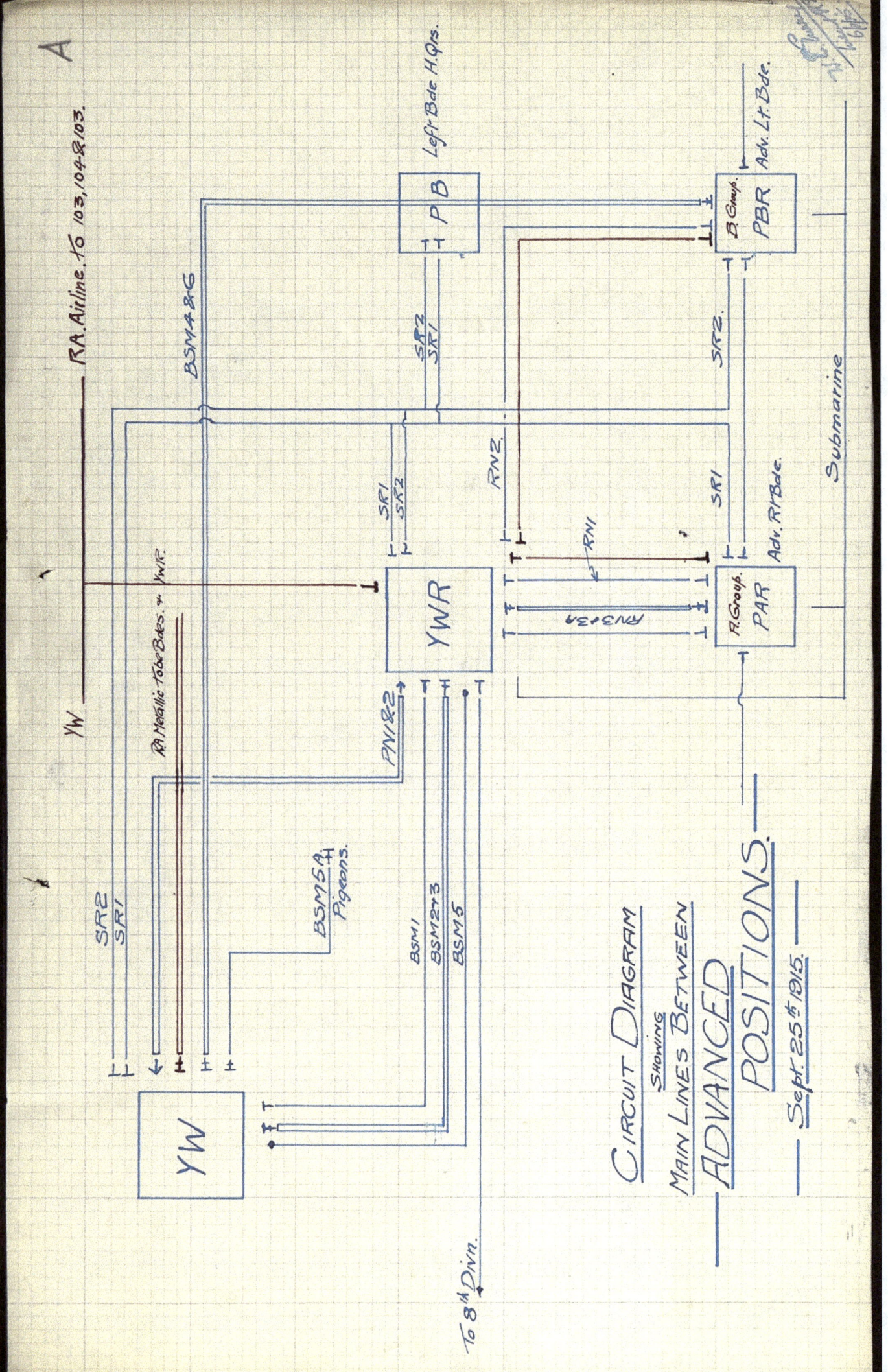

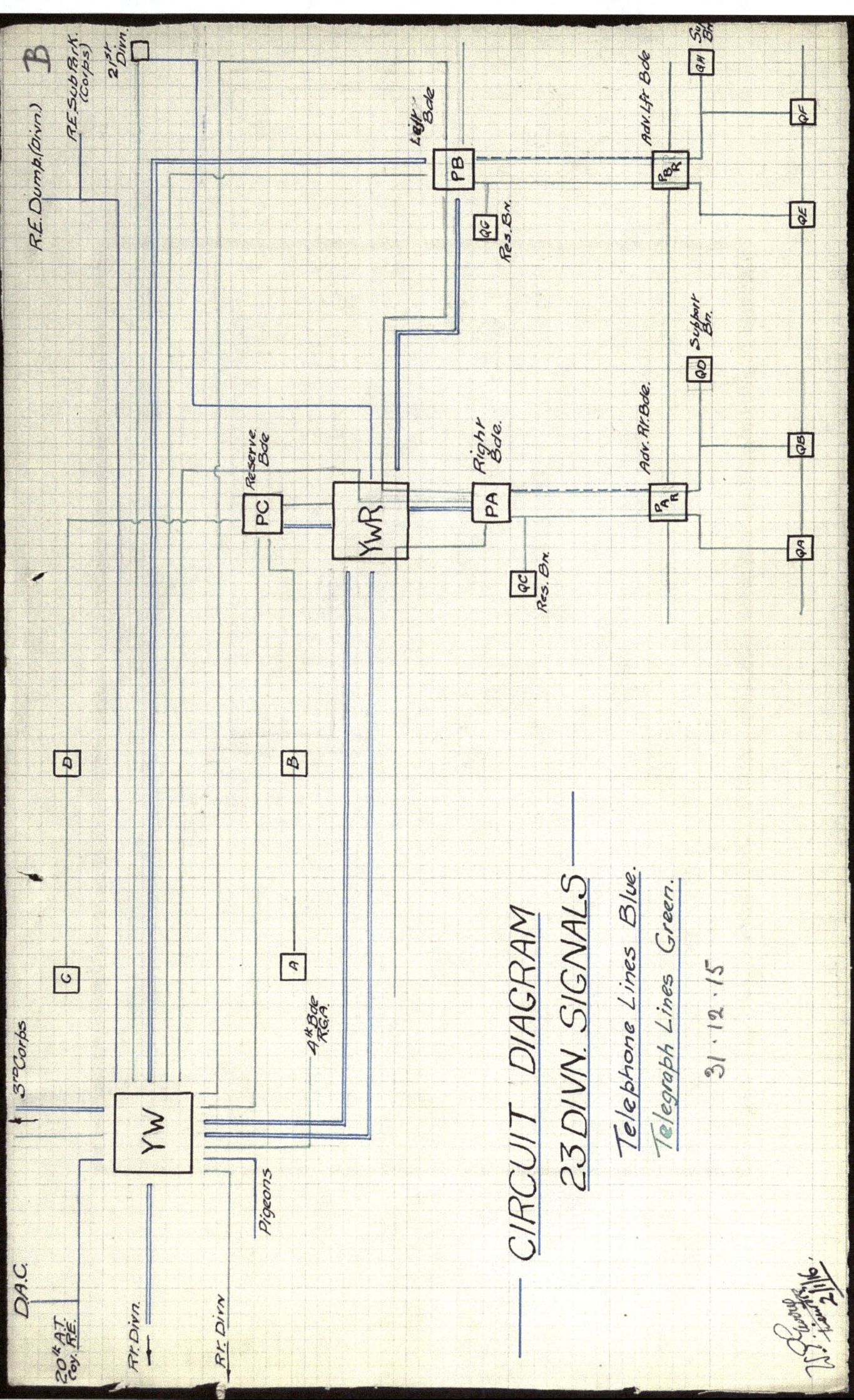

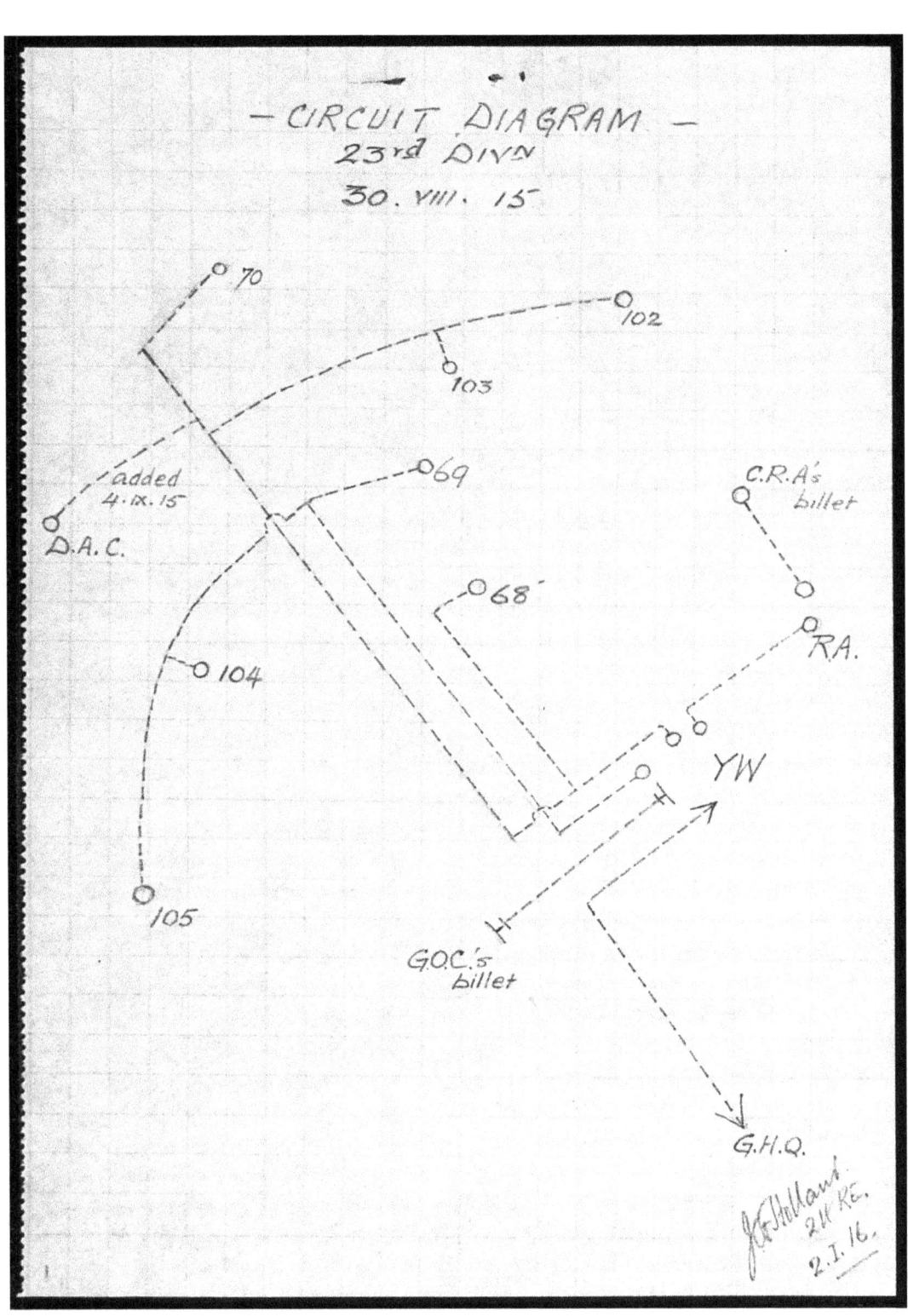

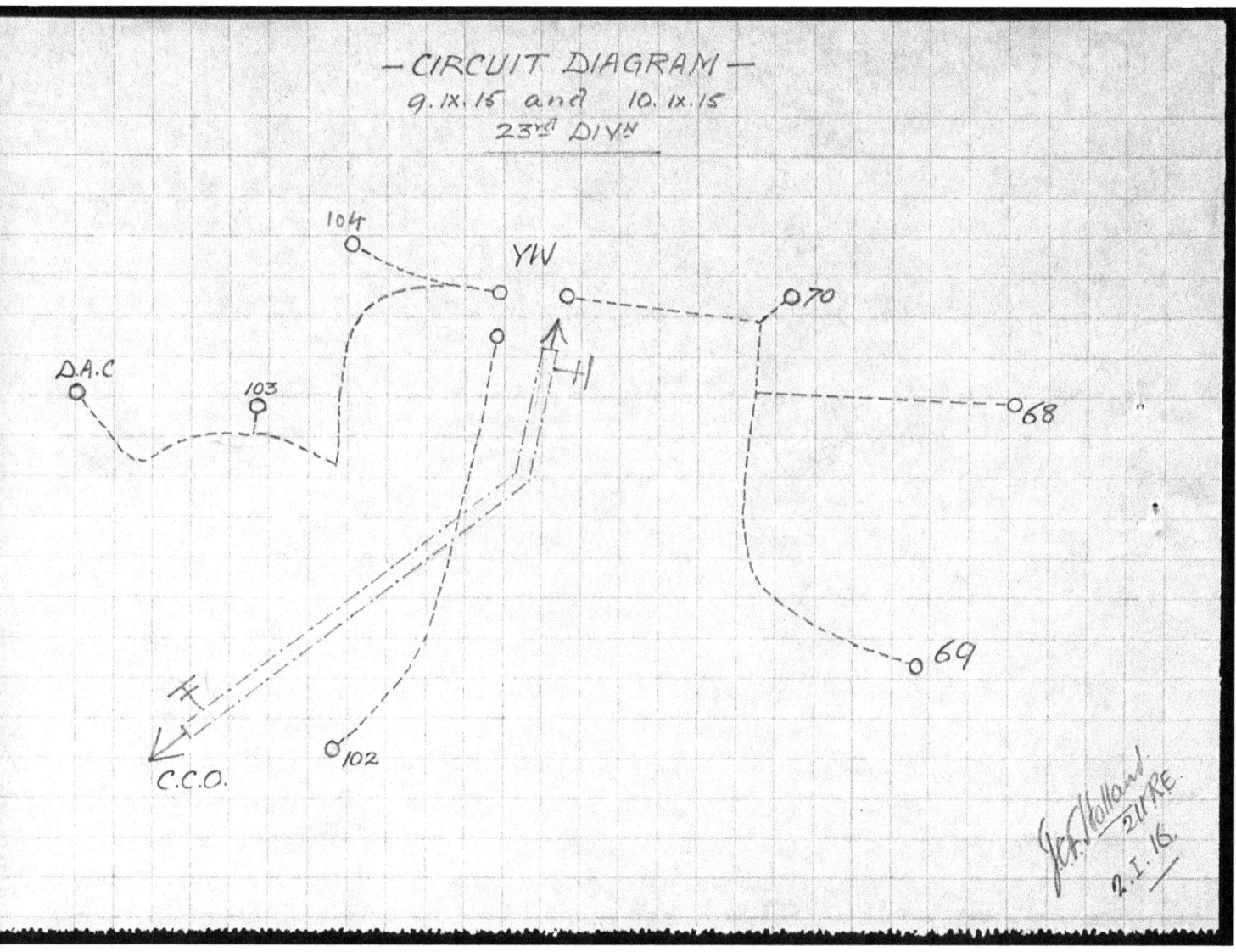

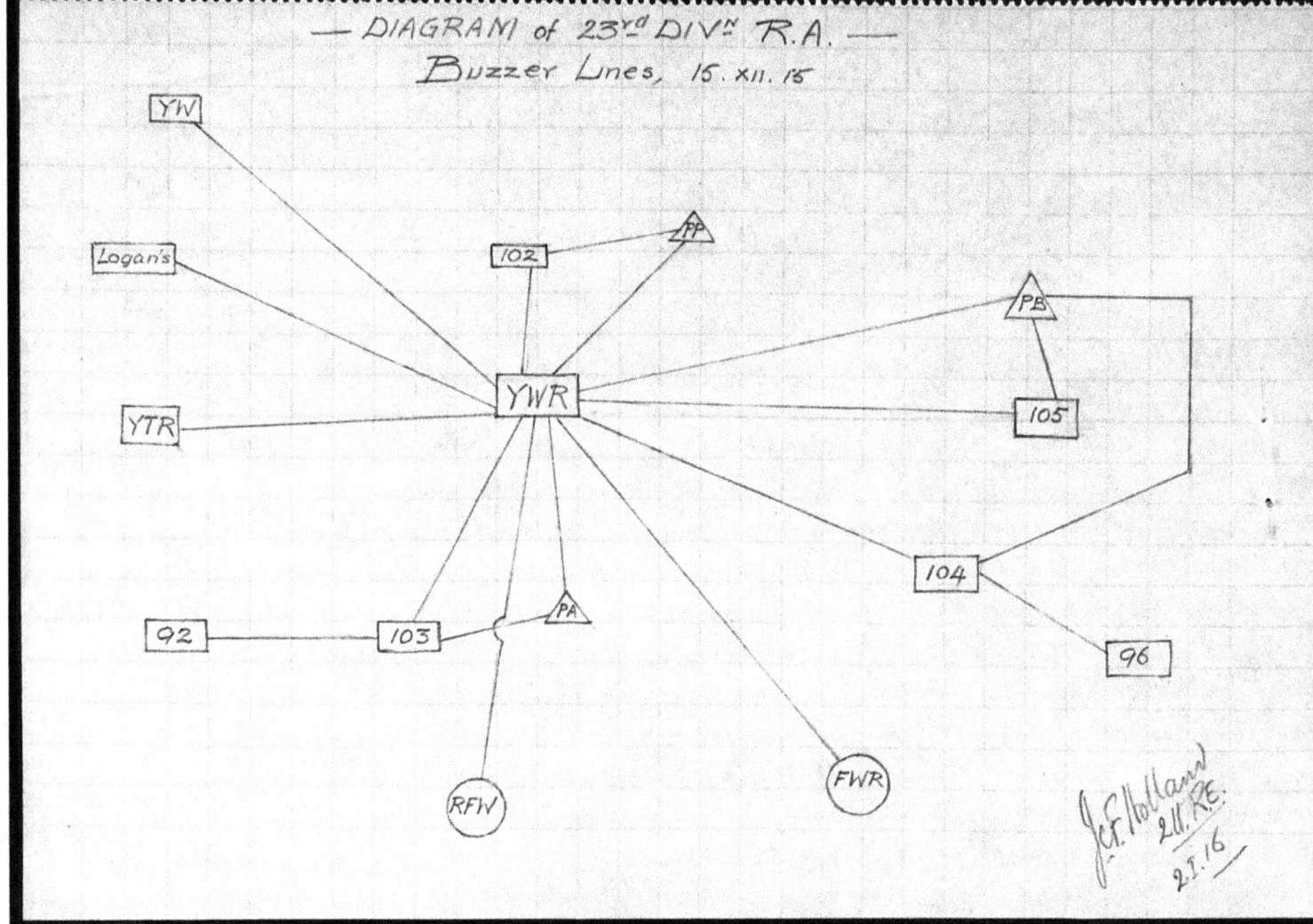

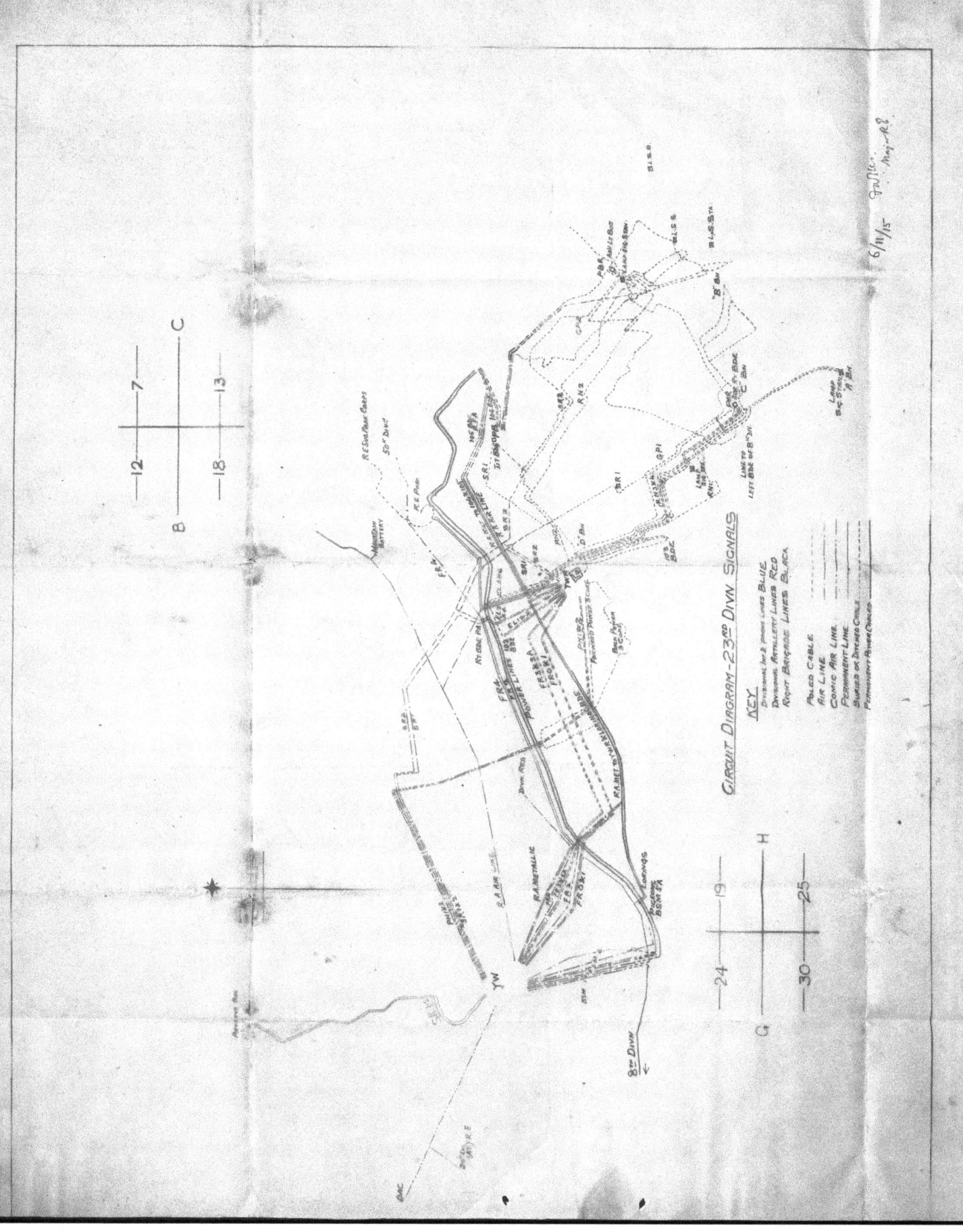

Army Form C. 2118.

WAR DIARY
or
INTELLIGENCE SUMMARY.

CONFIDENTIAL

War Diary
of
23rd Div'l Signal Coy R.E.
from Jan 1st 1916
to Feb 29th 1916

Gasler.
Maj. R.E.
O.C. 23rd Sig Co R.E.

29/2/16

Army Form C. 2118.

WAR DIARY
or
INTELLIGENCE SUMMARY.
(Erase heading not required.)

Place	Date 1916	Hour	Summary of Events and Information	Remarks and references to Appendices
CROIX DU BAC	1 Jan		Operating & Maintenance.	Jan
Do	2 Jan		Do	Jan
Do	3 Jan		Do	Jan
Do	4 Jan		Do. Erecting 4-line Cmie.	Jan
Do	5 Jan		Do. Erecting 4-line Cmie.	Jan
Do	6 Jan		Do. Erecting 4-line Cmie.	Jan
Do	7 Jan		Do. Erecting 4-line Cmie.	Jan
Do	8 Jan		Do. Nº 2 Sec. to ERQUINGHEM; Nº 4 Sec to ROLANDERIE.	Jan
Do	9 Jan		Do. Picked up FR 3 and 3A	Jan
Do	10 Jan		Do. Started 4 line Cmie to FORT ROMPU.	Jan
Do	11 Jan		Do. Erecting 4 line Cmie.	Jan
Do	12 Jan		Do. Erecting 4 line Cmie.	Jan
Do	13 Jan		Do. Erecting 4 line Cmie.	Jan

Army Form C. 2118.

WAR DIARY
or
INTELLIGENCE SUMMARY.
(Erase heading not required.)

Instructions regarding War Diaries and Intelligence Summaries are contained in F. S. Regs., Part II and the Staff Manual respectively. Title pages will be prepared in manuscript.

Place	Date	Hour	Summary of Events and Information	Remarks and references to Appendices
CROIX du BAC	14 Jan		Operating & Maintenance. Completed 4 line Circuit to FORT ROMPU	TM
Do	15 Jan		Do	TM
Do	16 Jan		Do	TM
Do	17 Jan		Do. Nº 2 Sec t RUE MARLE; Nº 3 Sec t ERQUINGHEM.	TM
Do	18 Jan		Do. 3 lines in tr ERQUINGHEM – ARMENTIÈRES road were cut by shell fire at 9 p.m.	TM
Do	19 Jan		Do. Very heavy TK rough at 11.15 p.m.	TM
Do	20 Jan		Do.	TM
Do	21 Jan		Do.	TM
Do	22 Jan		Do. 5F Buzzer Alarm Dismissed.	TM
Do	23 Jan		Do.	TM
Do	24 Jan		Do. Nº 3 Sec t ROLANTERIE; Nº 4 Sec t ERQUINGHEM.	TM
Do	25 Jan		Do.	TM
Do	26 Jan		Do. Reeling up	TM
Do	27 Jan		Do. Reeling up	TM

WAR DIARY
or
~~INTELLIGENCE SUMMARY~~

(Erase heading not required.)

Army Form C. 2118.

Place	Date	Hour	Summary of Events and Information	Remarks and references to Appendices
CROIX DU BAC	28 Jan		Operating & Maintenance. Started work on 8 line Circuit near FORT ROMPU	pm
do	29 Jan		Continued work on 8 line Circuit.	pm
do	30 Jan		Dismantling 4 line Circuit.	pm
do	31 Jan		N° 2 Sec t. ERQUINGHEM; N° 4 Sec. KRUE MARLE.	pm
do	1 Feb		(Party arrived from 34th Divisional Signal Coy for instruction)	pm
do	2 Feb		Erected Airline from JESUS Farm to 24 Bde Machine Gun.	pm
do	3 Feb		do	pm
do	4 Feb		do	pm
do	5 Feb		do	pm
do	6 Feb		do	pm
do	7 Feb		Electric Light plant & lorry arrived from AIRE.	pm
do	8 Feb		do	pm

WAR DIARY
or
INTELLIGENCE SUMMARY.
(Erase heading not required.)

Army Form C. 2118.

Place	Date	Hour	Summary of Events and Information	Remarks and references to Appendices
CROIX DU BAC	9 Feb		Operating & Maintenance. N° 2 Sec to RUE MARLE, N° 3 Sec to FERQUINGHEM	AM
Do	10 Feb		N° 3 Sec. left for STEENBECQUE in Reserve Area in relief of brigade of 34th Division (103rd Bde)	AM
Do	11 Feb		Burying cables behind ROLANDERIE & laid in all wires all FR lines near 101st FB Cy killed cut by shell-fire at 11.0 am & replaced, ; not-	AM
Do	12 Feb		Continued burying cables	AM
Do	13 Feb		Burying cables	AM
Do	14 Feb		Burying cables, infantry party assisting.	AM
Do	15 Feb		N° 4 Sec FERQUINGHEM. Burying cable at ROLANDERIE	AM
Do	16 Feb		N° 4 Sec. left for SERCUS in Reserve Area in relief of 102nd Bde.	AM
Do	17 Feb			AM
Do	18 Feb		Advance party of 34th Div. Signal Cy R.E. arrived	AM
Do	19 Feb			AM

WAR DIARY
or
INTELLIGENCE SUMMARY.
(Erase heading not required.)

Army Form C. 2118.

Instructions regarding War Diaries and Intelligence Summaries are contained in F.S. Regs., Part II. and the Staff Manual respectively. Title pages will be prepared in manuscript.

Place	Date	Hour	Summary of Events and Information	Remarks and references to Appendices
CROIX du BAC	20 Feb		Operating & Maintenance.	M
do	21 Feb		do	M
do	22 Feb		do	M
do	23 Feb		do	M
do	24 Feb	11 a.m.	Orders for BLARINGHEM cancelled. Closed at CROIX du BAC, re-opened at ESTAIRES.	M. DAJ
ESTAIRES	24 Feb		Ran a pair from Div HQ to LAVENTIE, utilizing P.O. lines via route Cornie to railway, thence along railway and Cornie to LAVENTIE.	M
do	25 Feb		Operating only.	M
BLARINGHEM	26 Feb		March to BLARINGHEM. Picked up LAVENTIE lines. Took over 3rd Corps Reserve Division lines on starting.	M Divn B
do	27 Feb		Operating only	M
do	28 Feb		Operating only	M
	29 Feb	9 a.m.	opened at BRUAY 10 a.m. closed at BLARINGHEM March to BRUAY. on transfer of 23rd Division from 3rd Corps 1st Army to 4th Corps 1st Army.	M
BRUAY				

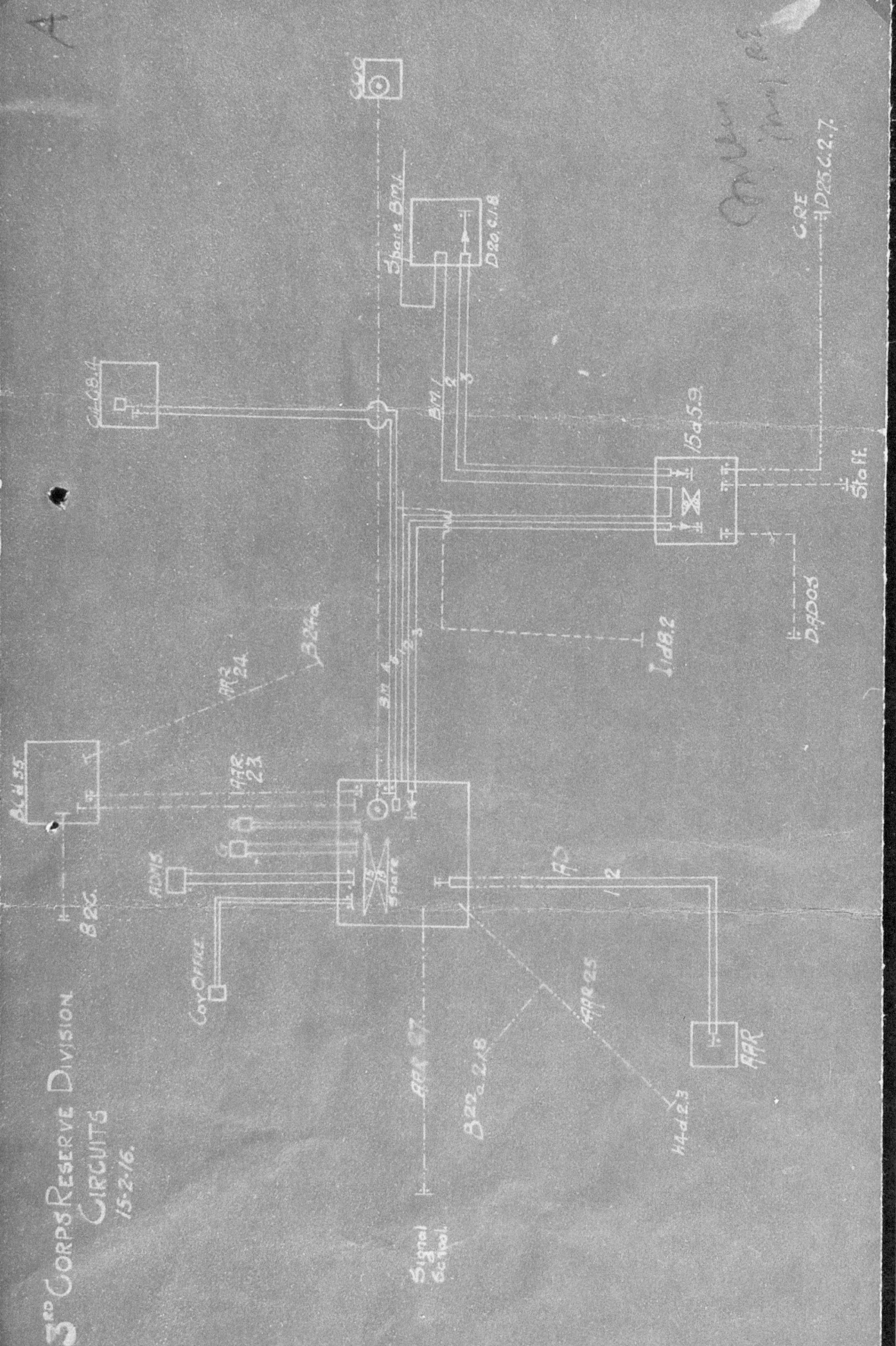

B

CIRCUIT DIAGRAM.
ESTAIRES
25.2.16

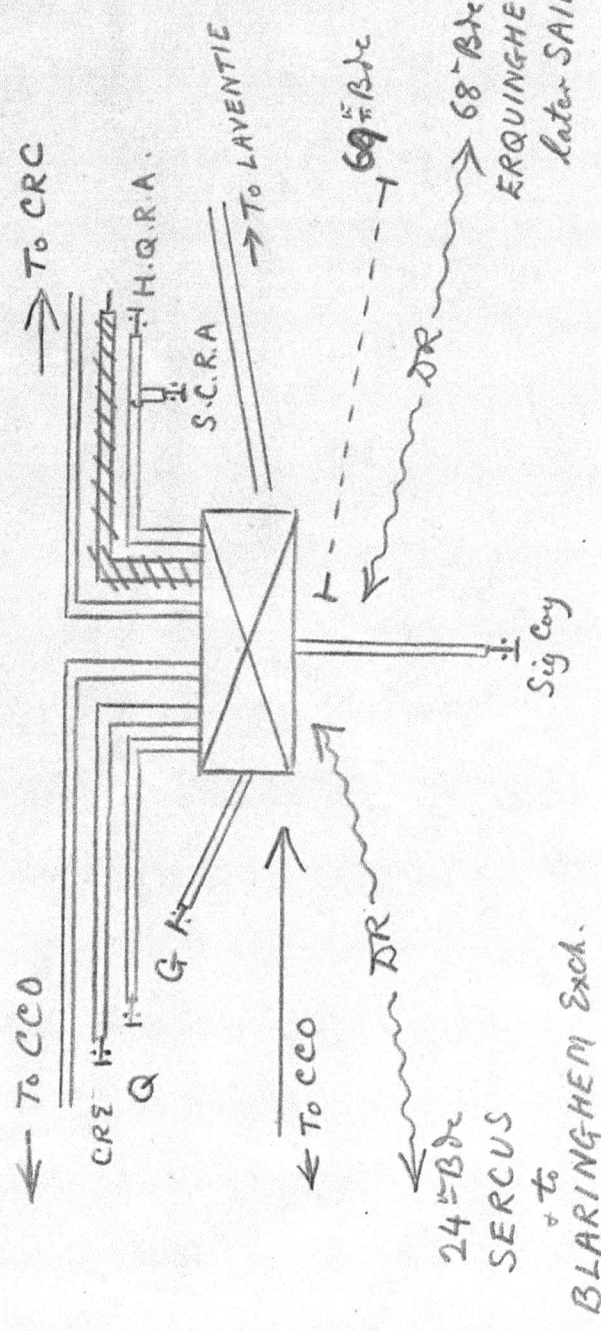

Jaller. Major R.S.
29/2/16

23 Div Signal
WR 4 and 5

Army Form C. 2118.

WAR DIARY
or
INTELLIGENCE SUMMARY.
(Erase heading not required.)

CONFIDENTIAL

War Diary
of
23rd Divn Signal Coy R.E.
from Mar 1st 1916
to April 30th 1916.

Tables.
9/5/16

Maj. R.E.
OC 23rd Sig Co R.E.

WAR DIARY
or
INTELLIGENCE SUMMARY.
(Erase heading not required.)

Army Form C. 2118.

Place	Date	Hour	Summary of Events and Information	Remarks and references to Appendices
BRUAY	1 Mar		Communication by D.R. Laid Cable to 69th Bde at RUITZ, teeing in to 24th Bde in BRUAY; laid cable at MARLY-les-MINES from IVth Corps Exchange to 68-73de	See plan A
do	2 Mar		Opened a D.R. Office at CAMBLAN-CHATELAIN. (Operating and Maintenance)	Fnl.
do	3 Mar		Operating and Maintenance	Fnl.
do	4 Mar		No 1 (1) Section complete to PETIT-SERVINS to lay Divisional lines in area now occupied by French 17th Division. Operating and Maintenance.	Fnl.
and PETIT-SERVINS BRUAY & PTT-SERVINS	5 Mar		Operating and Maintenance.	
ditto	6 Mar		Operating and Maintenance.	
ditto	7 Mar		Operating and Maintenance.	
Chau de la HAIE and PTT-SERVINS	8 Mar		Closed Office at 10 a.m. and opened at Chateau de la HAIE at 10 a.m. in relief of French 17th Division. Operating & Maintenance.	See plans B1. Fnl. B2
ditto	9 Mar		"AW" Cable Section from IVth Corps arrived at PETIT-SERVINS to assist. Operating and Maintenance.	Fnl
ditto	10 Mar		Continued line to O.C. Train at MAISNIL BOUCHIE to Adm.S. and RADIOS. AW Section laid Cable to meet 2nd Division on left.	Fnl.

WAR DIARY
INTELLIGENCE SUMMARY.
(Erase heading not required.)

Army Form C. 2118.

Place	Date	Hour	Summary of Events and Information	Remarks and references to Appendices
Chau de la HAIE	11 Mar		Operating & Maintenance. Connected S.C. of brigade in the line from GOUY-SERVINS to Bde HQ at ABLAIN-ST-NAZAIRE; ran cable from ABLAIN-ST-NAZAIRE through BOIS de BOUVIGNY to join up with brigade on left.	M.
Do	12 Mar		Operating & Maintenance. Put D.A.C. at CAUCOURT through to ESTREE-CAUCHIE (permant line) and from manuat to Div. HQ	M.
Do	13 Mar		Operating & Maintenance. Cable to 81st Siege Battery from D in HQ and to R.M.A. Hermitage at VILLERS AW Section put through PA 1 and 2 on French aerial poles; replaced cable by cessie airline between YW and PB and upon 2 lines from RANCHI-COURT and 2 lines from FRESNICOURT. Sapper Clarke C.H. was killed by an aerial torpedo at SOUCHEZ.	M.
Do	14 Mar		Operating & Maintenance	M.
Do	15 Mar		Operating & Maintenance	M.
BRUAY	16 Mar		Returned to BRUAY on relief by 47th Division. Office closed at Ch. de la HAIE at 10 am and opened at BRUAY same time	See plan C M.
Do	17 Mar		Operating & Maintenance.	M.
Do	18 Mar		Operating & Maintenance.	M.
Do	19 Mar		Operating & Maintenance.	M.
Do	20 Mar		Operating & Maintenance	M.

Army Form C. 2118.

WAR DIARY
or
INTELLIGENCE SUMMARY.
(Erase heading not required.)

Instructions regarding War Diaries and Intelligence Summaries are contained in F. S. Regs., Part II. and the Staff Manual respectively. Title pages will be prepared in manuscript.

Place	Date	Hour	Summary of Events and Information	Remarks and references to Appendices
BRUAY	21 Mar		Operating and Maintenance.	App.2
SAINS-en-GOHELLE	22 Mar		Marched to SAINS in relief of 2nd Division; offices closed; opened at 10. a.m. No 2 and 3 Sections at BULLY; No 4 at AIX-NOULETTE; took over 2 wireless stations kept by 2nd Div. at all lines. Laid cable from BULLY to AIX.	App1 See plans App1 FDS
Do	23 Mar		Operating and Maintenance.	App1
Do	24 Mar		Laid cable from R.A.H.Q. at BOYEFFLES to right and left groups. (100 Infantry burying cable at night.)	App1
Do	25 Mar		Operating and Maintenance.	App1
Do	26 Mar		100 Infantry burying cable at night.	App1
Do	27 Mar		Laid cable from R.A.H.Q. to 49th Siege Battery.	App1
Do	28 Mar		Operating and Maintenance. Four wireless sets received and established at Notre Dame de LORETTE, BOUVIGNY, SAINS and CALONNE; Taken over left by 2nd Div. being with drawn. Relaying line to Advanced 1st Division.	App1
Do	29 Mar		Operating and Maintenance. 6" Infantry Buzzer-Class started instruction.	App1
Do	30 Mar		Operating and Maintenance. Relaid line & rodded up old line 67th Division.	App1
Do	31 Mar		Operating and Maintenance. Replacing poled cable by airline (armoured) between Div HQ & BULLY	App1

WAR DIARY
INTELLIGENCE SUMMARY.
(Erase heading not required.)

Army Form C. 2118.

Place	Date	Hour	Summary of Events and Information	Remarks and references to Appendices
SAINS-en-GOHELLE	1 Apr		Operating and Maintenance.	Replacing poled cable by cervice air line between SAINS and BULLY. Cavalry party 280 strong burying cable	M
Do	2 Apr		Operating and Maintenance.	Making B 30 and B 12 metallic.	M
Do	3 Apr		Operating and Maintenance.	Making lines metallic between SAINS and BULLY.	M
Do	4 Apr		Operating and Maintenance.	Started poling B 19, B 25 & B 26.	M
Do	5 Apr		Operating and Maintenance.	Completed B 19 and reeled up old cable.	M
Do	6 Apr		Operating and Maintenance.	Poling cable.	M
Do	7 Apr		Operating and Maintenance.	Poling cable.	M
Do	8 Apr		Operating and Maintenance.	Reeling up old cable and poling B 2.	M
Do	9 Apr		Operating and Maintenance.		M
Do	10 Apr		Operating and Maintenance.	Replacing B 2 by open wire; jointing buried cable.	M

Army Form C. 2118.

WAR DIARY
or
INTELLIGENCE SUMMARY.
(Erase heading not required.)

Instructions regarding War Diaries and Intelligence Summaries are contained in F. S. Regs., Part II. and the Staff Manual respectively. Title pages will be prepared in manuscript.

Place	Date	Hour	Summary of Events and Information	Remarks and references to Appendices
SAINS-en-GOHELLE	11 Apr		Operating and Maintenance. Connecting field cable into open-line	App
Do	12 Apr		Operating and Maintenance. Connecting B25	App
Do	13 Apr		Operating and Maintenance. Started overhauling B30, B31 and B33	App
Do	14 Apr		Operating and Maintenance. Visual - class of 16 infantry formed	App
Do	15 Apr		Operating and Maintenance	App
Do	16 Apr		Operating and Maintenance. Re-constructing lines between BULLY and AIX-NOULETTE	App
Do	17 Apr		Operating and Maintenance.	App
Do	18 Apr		Operating and Maintenance.	App
BRUAY	19 Apr		Went into GHQ Reserve at BRUAY on relief by 2nd Division; offices changed at 10 a.m.	App
Do	20 Apr		Operating and Maintenance.	App

WAR DIARY
or
INTELLIGENCE SUMMARY.
(Erase heading not required.)

Army Form C. 2118.

Instructions regarding War Diaries and Intelligence Summaries are contained in F. S. Regs., Part II. and the Staff Manual respectively. Title pages will be prepared in manuscript.

Place	Date	Hour	Summary of Events and Information	Remarks and references to Appendices
BRUAY	20 Apr		Operating and Maintenance.	JM
Do	21 Apr		Operating and Maintenance. Started Field Training – also Drill	JM
Do	22 Apr		Operating and Maintenance.	JM
Do	23 Apr		Operating and Maintenance.	JM
Do	24 Apr		Operating and Maintenance.	JM
Do	25 Apr		Operating and Maintenance. 6" Buzzer – Class (24 NCOs of ? 12 mos) Examined.	JM
Do	26 Apr		Operating and Maintenance. 7" Buzzer – Class (68 & 69 Tres of ? 16 mm) joined.	JM
Do	27 Apr		Operating and Maintenance. Established Visual communication between Div HQ (BRUAY) and Bde HQ (DIV ON). Running daily from 9.0 am. 9.0 pm.	JM
Do	28 Apr		Operating and Maintenance.	JM
Do	29 Apr		Operating and Maintenance.	JM
Do	30 Apr		Operating and Maintenance.	JM

CIRCUIT DIAGRAM
23rd Div.
29.2.16

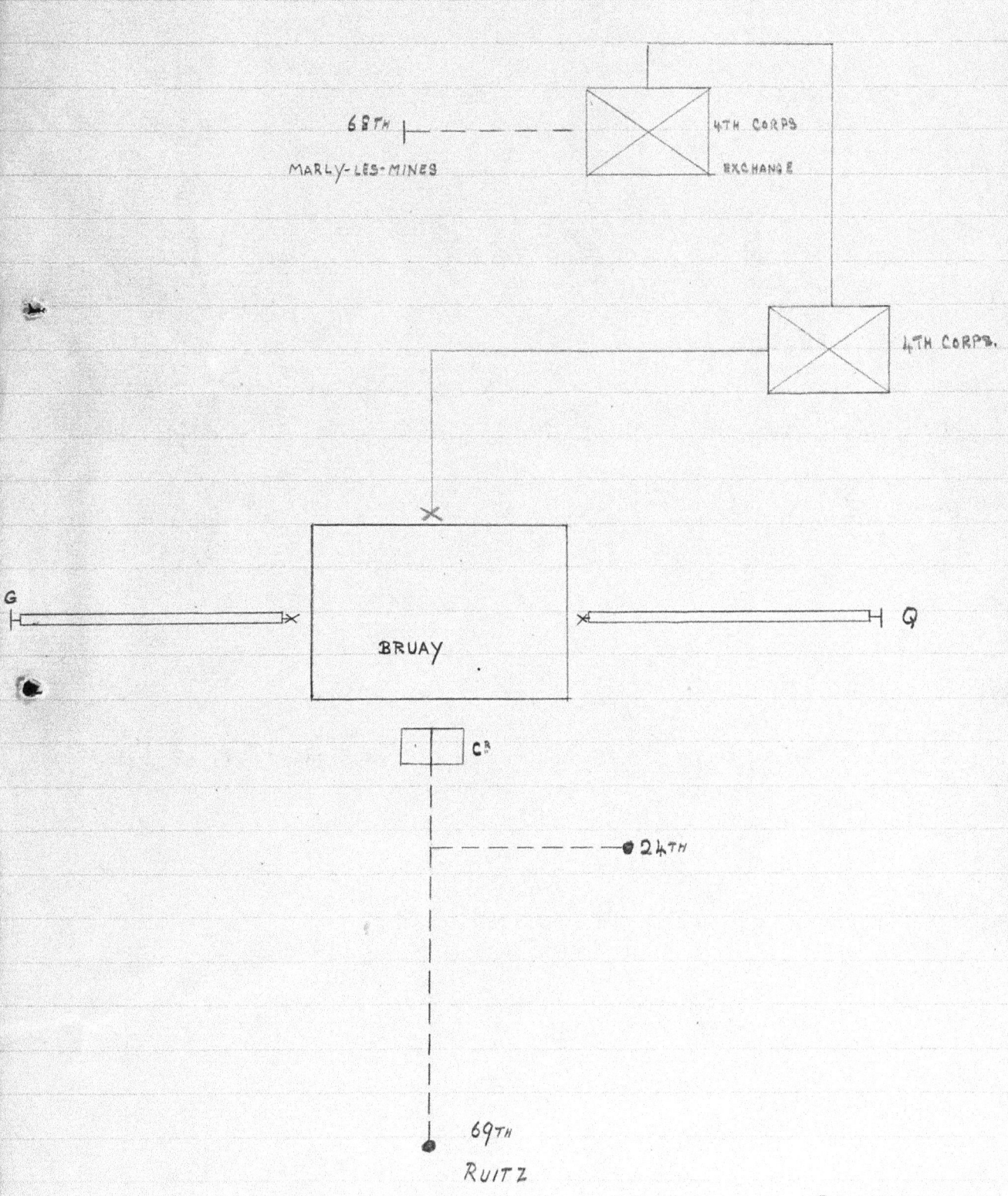

B1

CIRCUIT DIAGRAM.
12.3.16

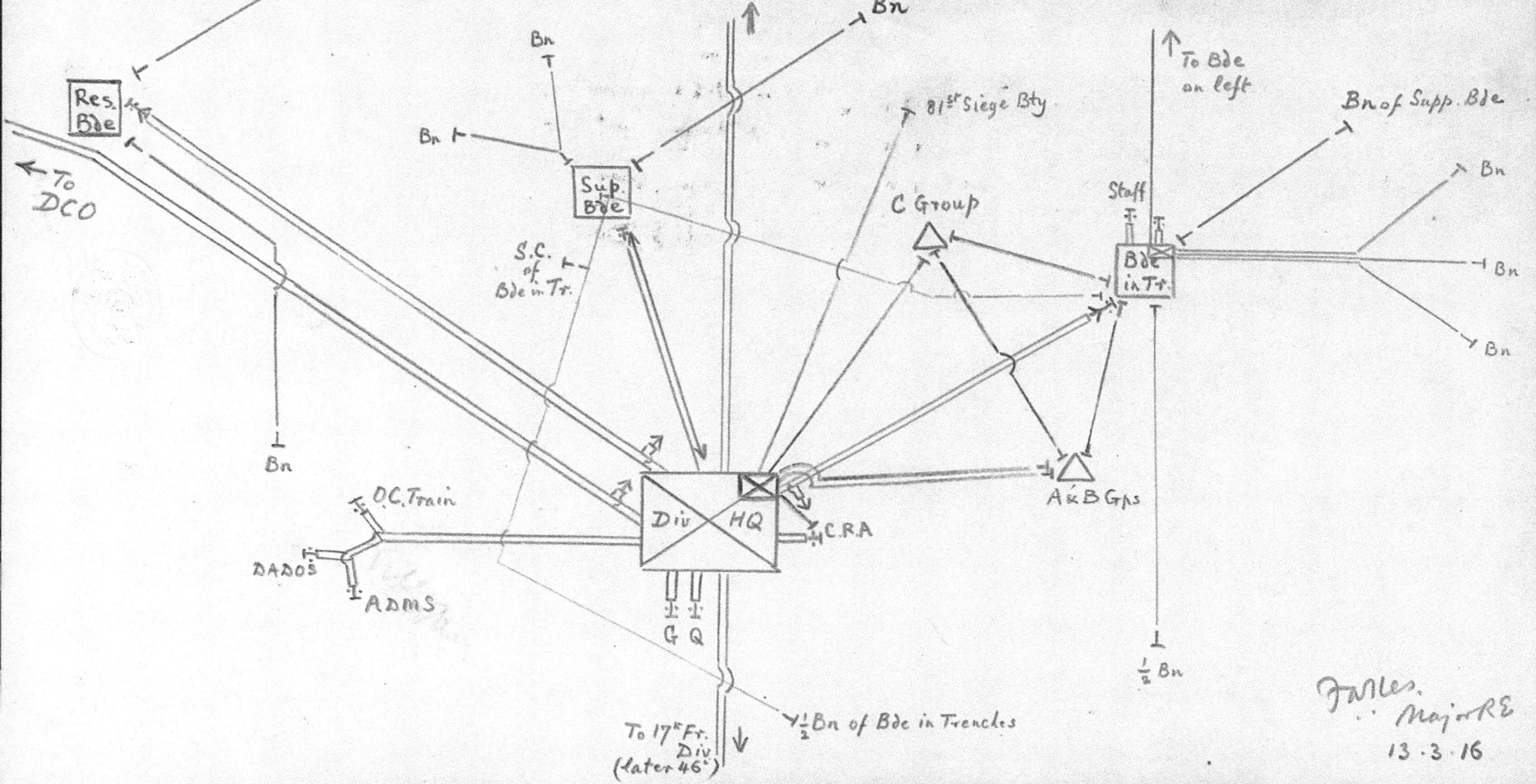

Tyler. Major RE
13.3.16

↑ To Bde on left

Bn of Supp. Bde

Bn
Bn
Bn

Staff — Bde in Tr.

½ Bn

A & B Gps

C Group

81st Siege Bty

CRA

Bn

To 2nd Div ←

HQ Div

½ Bn of Bde in Trenches

G Q

To 17th Ft. Div (later 46) →

Sup. Bde

S.C. of Bde in Tr.

Bn
Bn

O.C. Train

DADOS ADMS

Bn

Bn

Res. Bde

To DCO ↓

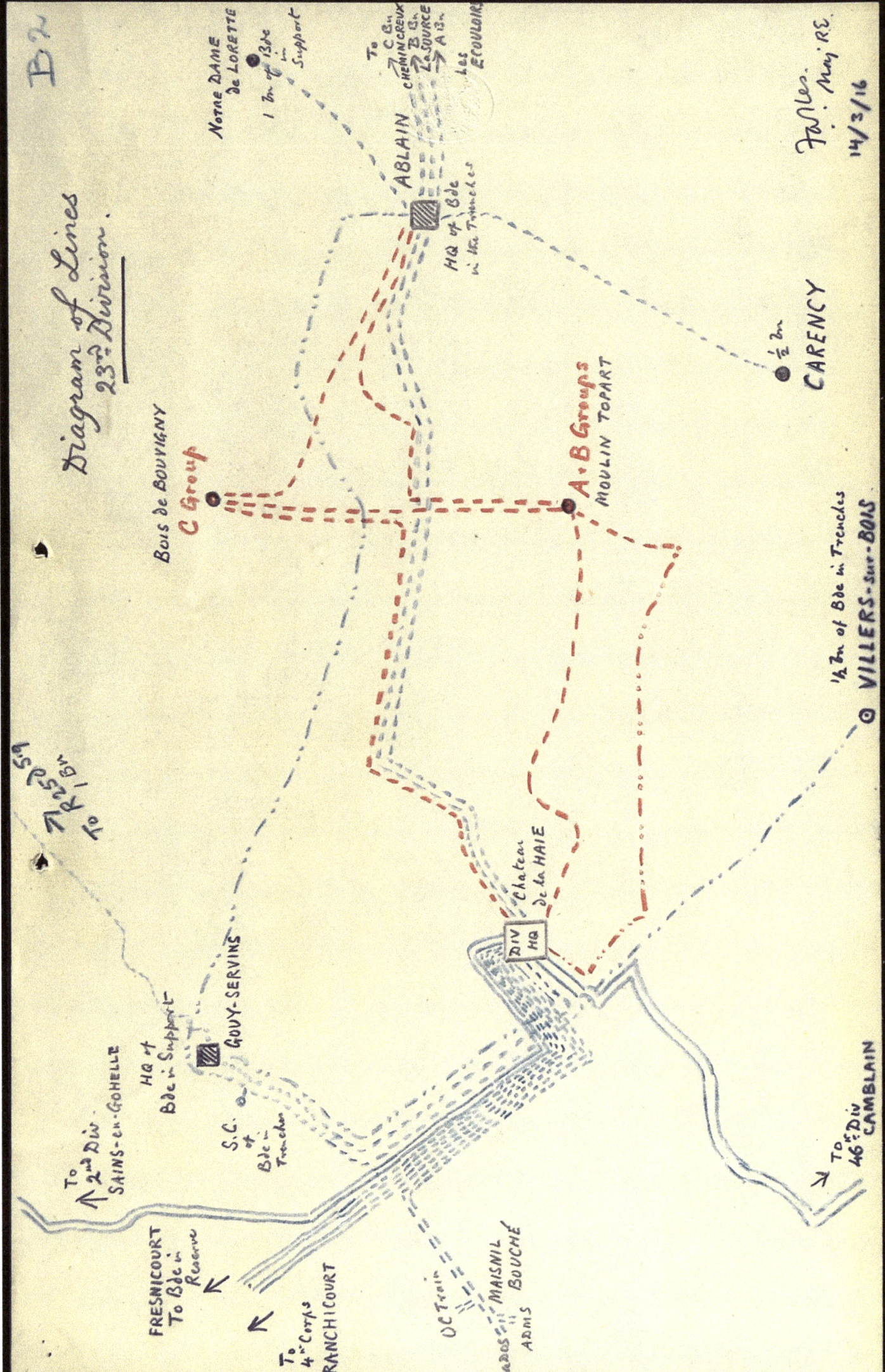

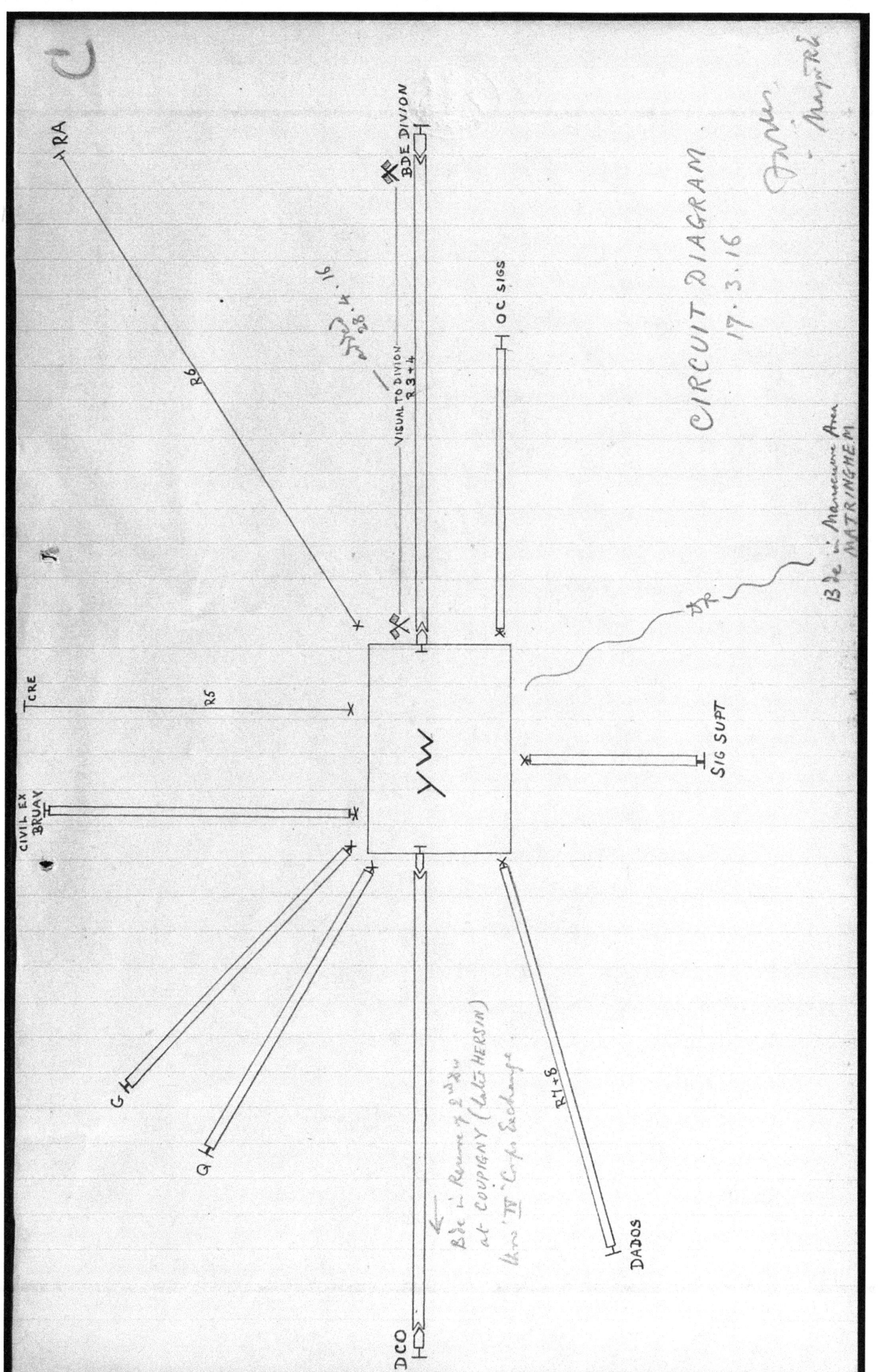

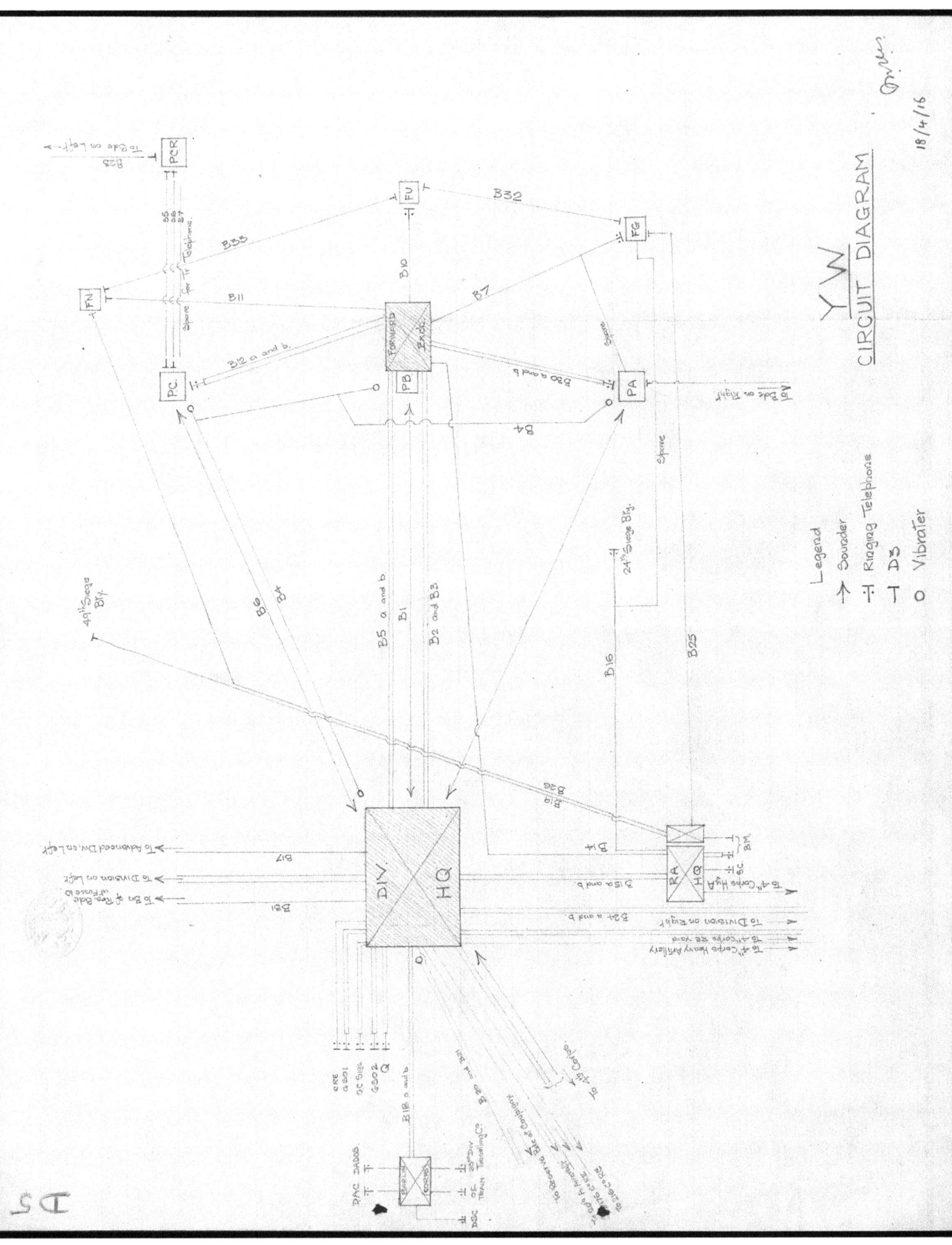

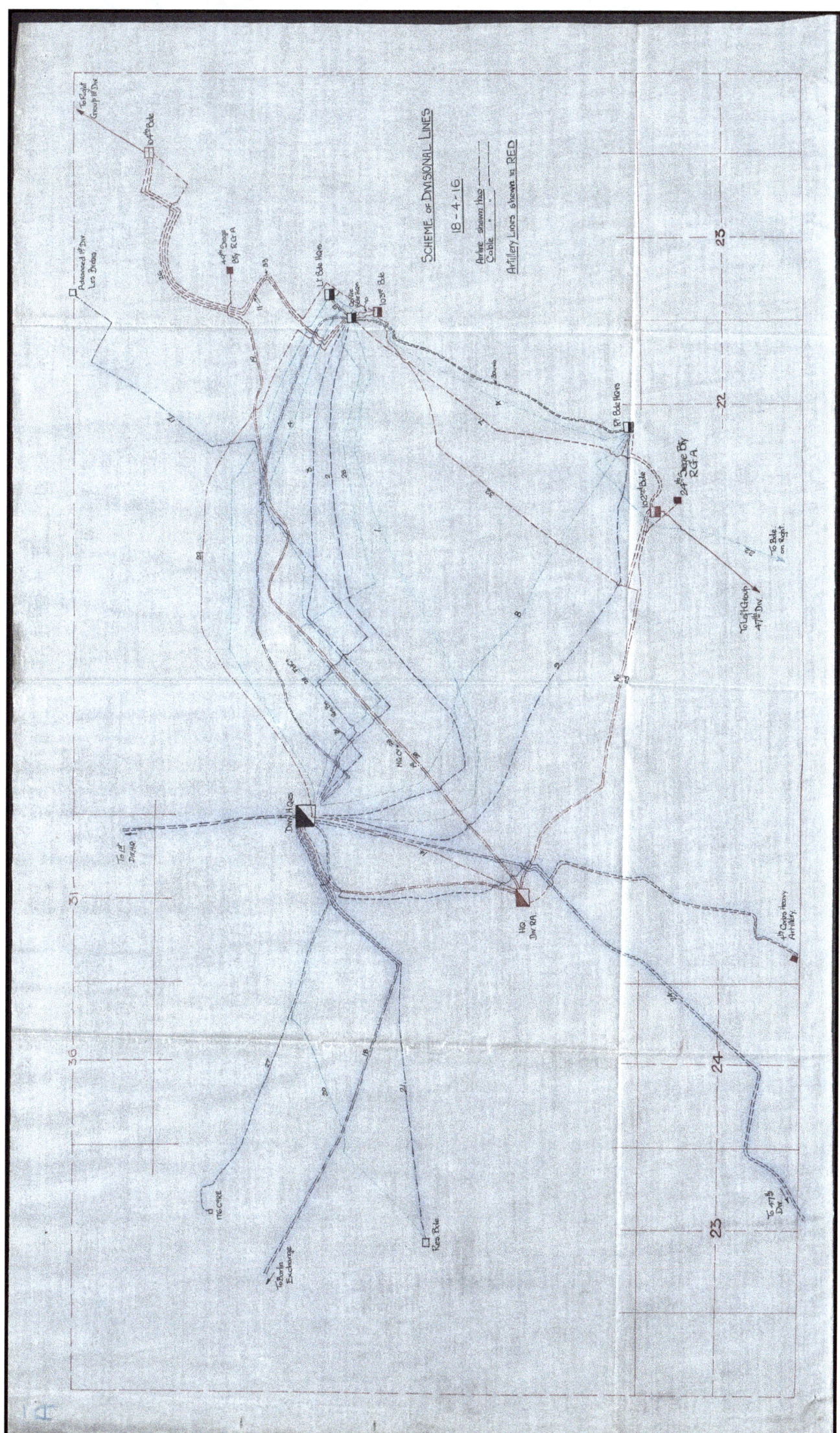

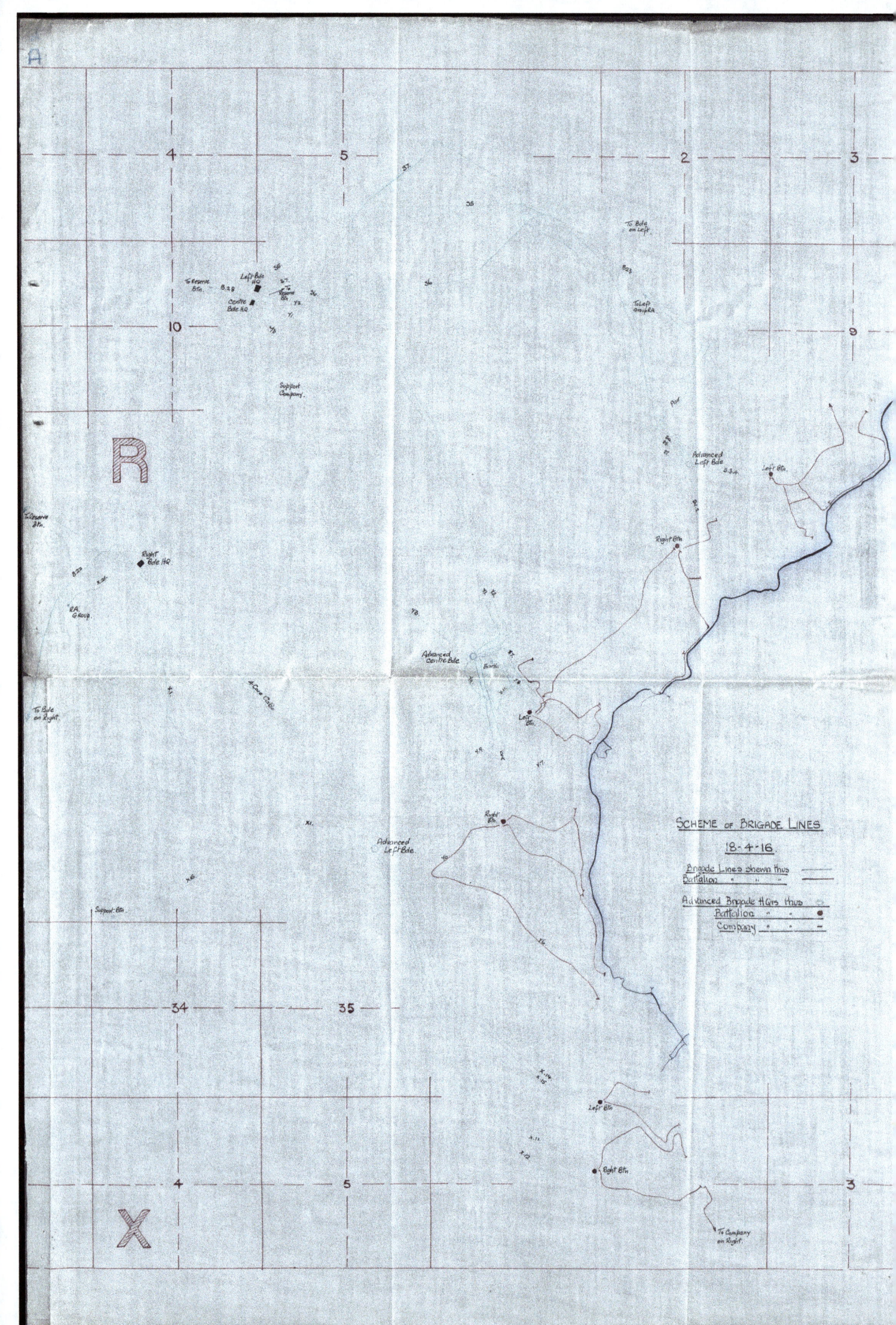

WAR DIARY
or
INTELLIGENCE SUMMARY.

Army Form C. 2118.

CONFIDENTIAL.

War Diary
of
23rd Div./55 Signal Coy R.E.
for
May 1916

Fraser
Maj. R.E.
O.C. 23rd Div Sig. Coy R.E.
6/6/16

WAR DIARY
or
INTELLIGENCE SUMMARY.
(Erase heading not required.)

Army Form C. 2118.

Place	Date	Hour	Summary of Events and Information	Remarks and references to Appendices
BRUAY	1 May		Head Quarters and No 1 in GHQ Reserve; No 4 Sec with 24" Bde in Manoeuvre Area at MATRINGHEM; No 3 Sec with 69" Bde at HERSIN acting as Reserve Bde to 2"D Div. No 2 Sec with 68" Bde at DIVION, resting. Operating, Maintenance; Training in Cable-Drill and visual.	M.
BRUAY	2 May		Operating & Maintenance. Training in Wagon Cable-Drill & Visual.	M
BRUAY	3 May		Operating & Maintenance Training in Wagon Cable-Drill & Visual	M
BRUAY	4 May		Operating & Maintenance. Visual-training, riding-drill.	M
BRUAY	5 May		Operating & Maintenance Visual Training, riding-drill	M
BRUAY	6 May		Operating & Maintenance Visual Training, riding-drill	M.
BRUAY	7 May		Operating & Maintenance Visual training	M
BRUAY	8 May		Operating & Maintenance Visual training & riding-drill.	M
BRUAY	9 May		Operating, Maintenance & Visual Training	M.

Army Form C. 2118.

WAR DIARY
or
INTELLIGENCE SUMMARY.
(Erase heading not required.)

Instructions regarding War Diaries and Intelligence Summaries are contained in F. S. Regs., Part II. and the Staff Manual respectively. Title pages will be prepared in manuscript.

Place	Date	Hour	Summary of Events and Information	Remarks and references to Appendices
BRUAY	10 May	/	Operating & Maintenance	Jm
BRUAY	11 May	/	Operating & Maintenance. Did a scheme near HOUDAIN, signals only with G.S. advance and relievement of 2 brigades.	Jm
BRUAY	12 May	/	Operating & Maintenance	Jm
SAINS-en-GOHELLE	13 May	/	Moved into the line relieving 2nd Division; took over 3 Bde-fronts, as follows :- SOUCHEZ section, 24th Bde.; ANGRES section, 69th Bde.; CALONNE section, 6th Bde (left by 2nd Div) : 68th Bde at MATRINGHEM (Manoeuvre Area).	Jm
do	14 May	/	Operating & Maintenance	Jm
do	15 May	/	Operating & Maintenance	m.
do	16 May	/	Operating & Maintenance.	m
do	17 May	/	Operating & Maintenance.	m
do	18 May	/	CALONNE Section handed over to 1st Div (1st Bde), reducing us to 2-Bde front. Operating & Maintenance.	m
do	19 May	/	Operating & Maintenance. No 2 Sec from MATRINGHEM to FRESNICOURT.	m
do	20 May	/	Operating & Maintenance	Jm

WAR DIARY
or
INTELLIGENCE SUMMARY.

Army Form C. 2118.

Place	Date	Hour	Summary of Events and Information	Remarks and references to Appendices
SAINS-en-GOHELLE	21 May		No 2 & AIX-NOULETTE, No 4 & FRESNICOURT	
			Operating & Maintenance. The following lines cut by shell-fire; — (Divisional) B 2, B3, B4, B7, B8, B9, (RA) B 16 (pair) and B42, (Inter-brigade) B30 (pair)	M
do	22 May		Operating & Maintenance. Re-laid & replace destroyed lines: — B7 and B 30 (single). Lines cut by shell-fire B1, B4, B7 (twice) B17, B.30. At 7.0 pm all lines were through for the first time since 2.30 pm 21st (28½ hours) No 4 & HERSIN.	M
do	23 May		Operating & Maintenance. Lines cut by shell-fire B1, B4, B6, B9, B18, B30, B40 & B42.	M
do	24 May		Operating & Maintenance. Lines cut by shell-fire B1, B4, B8, B9, B15 (pair) B40, B41 (pair) DCO	M
do	25 May		SAINS shelled. Dvr Mitchell killed by shrapnel & 2 horses wounded.	M
do	26 May		Operating & Maintenance.	M
do	27 May		Operating & Maintenance.	M
do	28 May		Operating & Maintenance. 7F Bugger-Class Joining. Skates 8-line Cmie.	M
do	29 May		Operating & Maintenance. Erecting 8-line Cmie as part of new scheme.	M
do	30 May		Operating & Maintenance. Sent back to BARLIN, CSM, CQMS, 3 NCOs 3 Sappers, all Drivers except 4 & Bugger-class (60 men) joined on Scheme & maintenance. 68 horses and all wagons but 3 for work on Scheme & maintenance.	M
do	31 May		Operating & Maintenance. No 4 Sec to BULLY-GRENAY, No 3 Sec to HERSIN	M

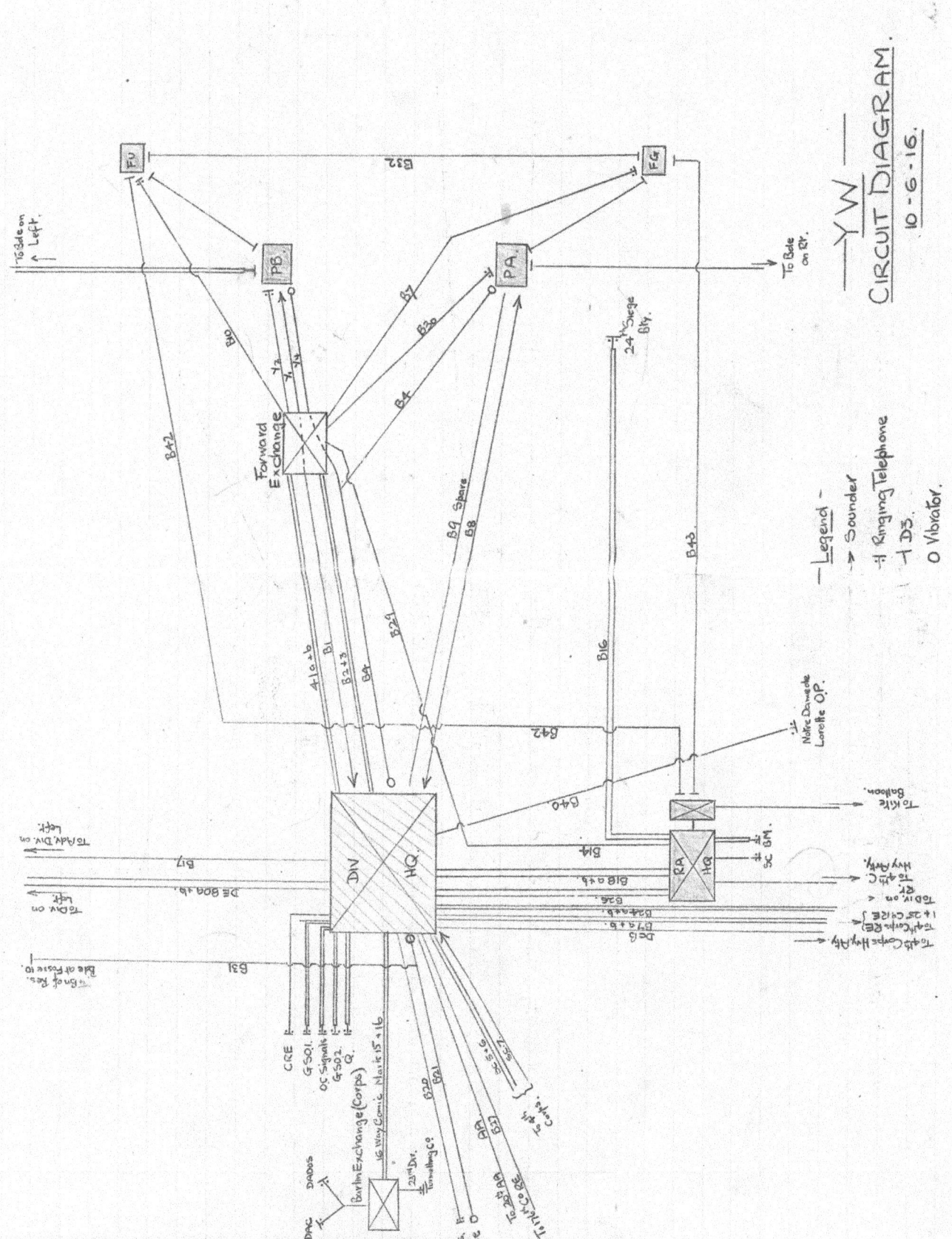

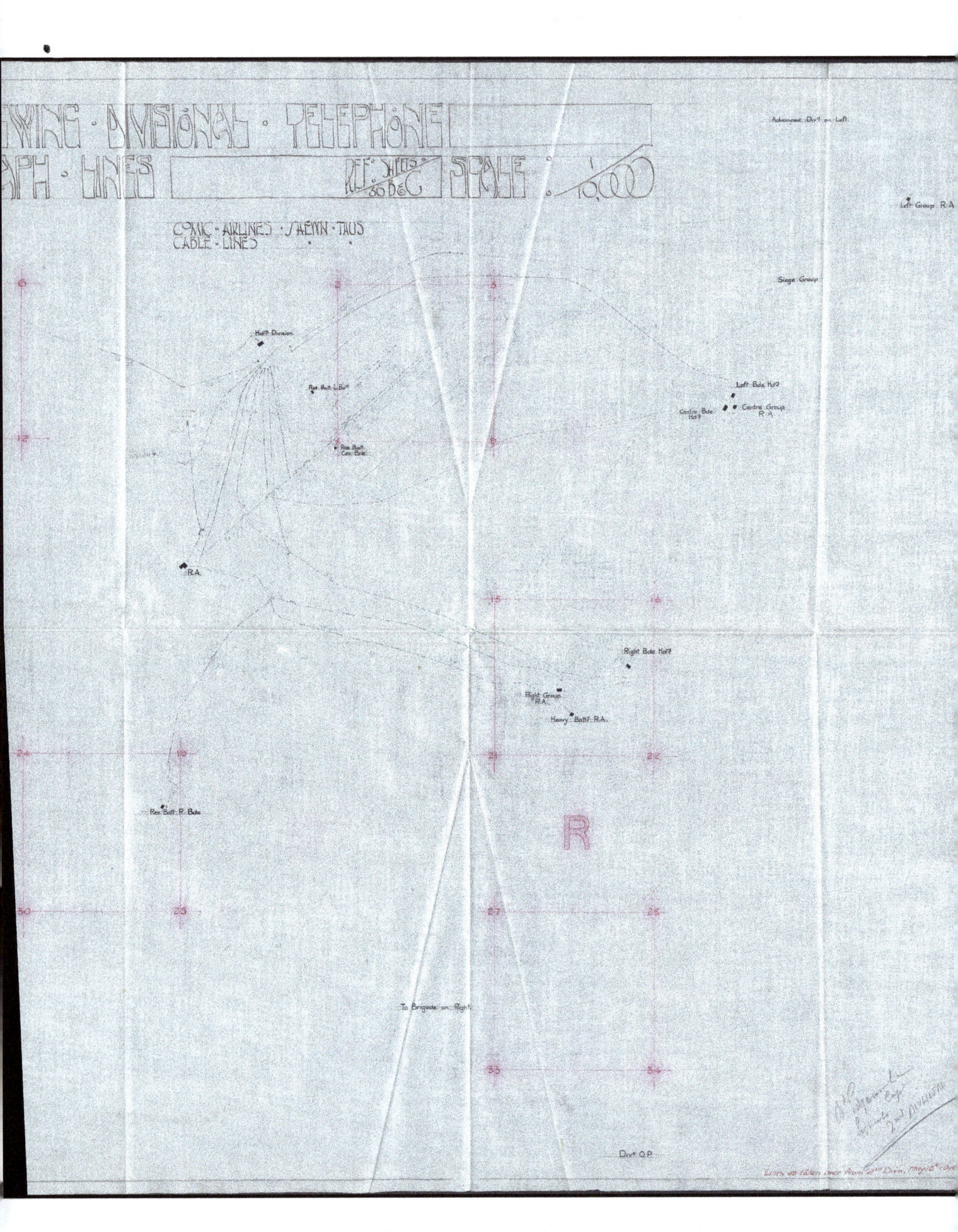

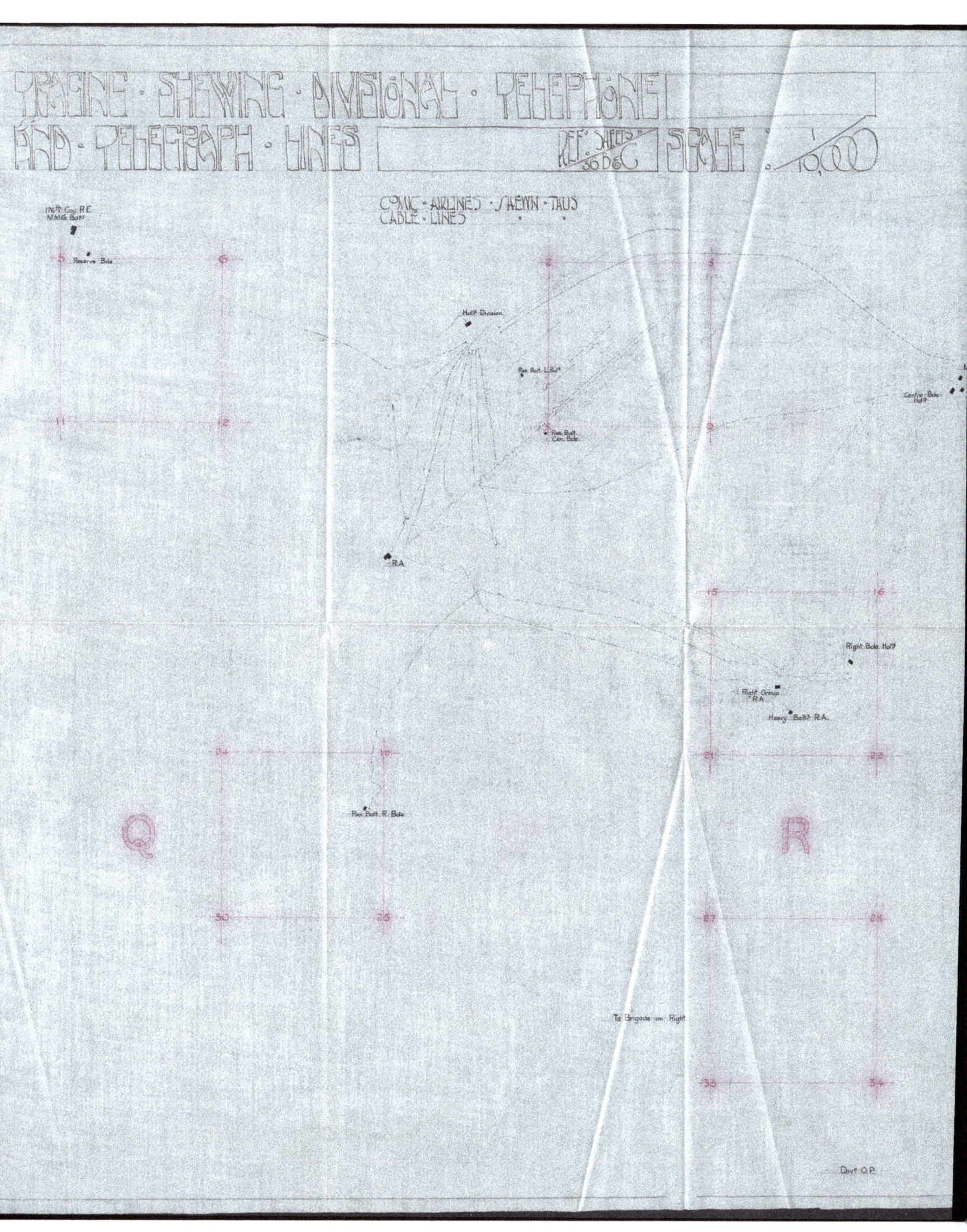

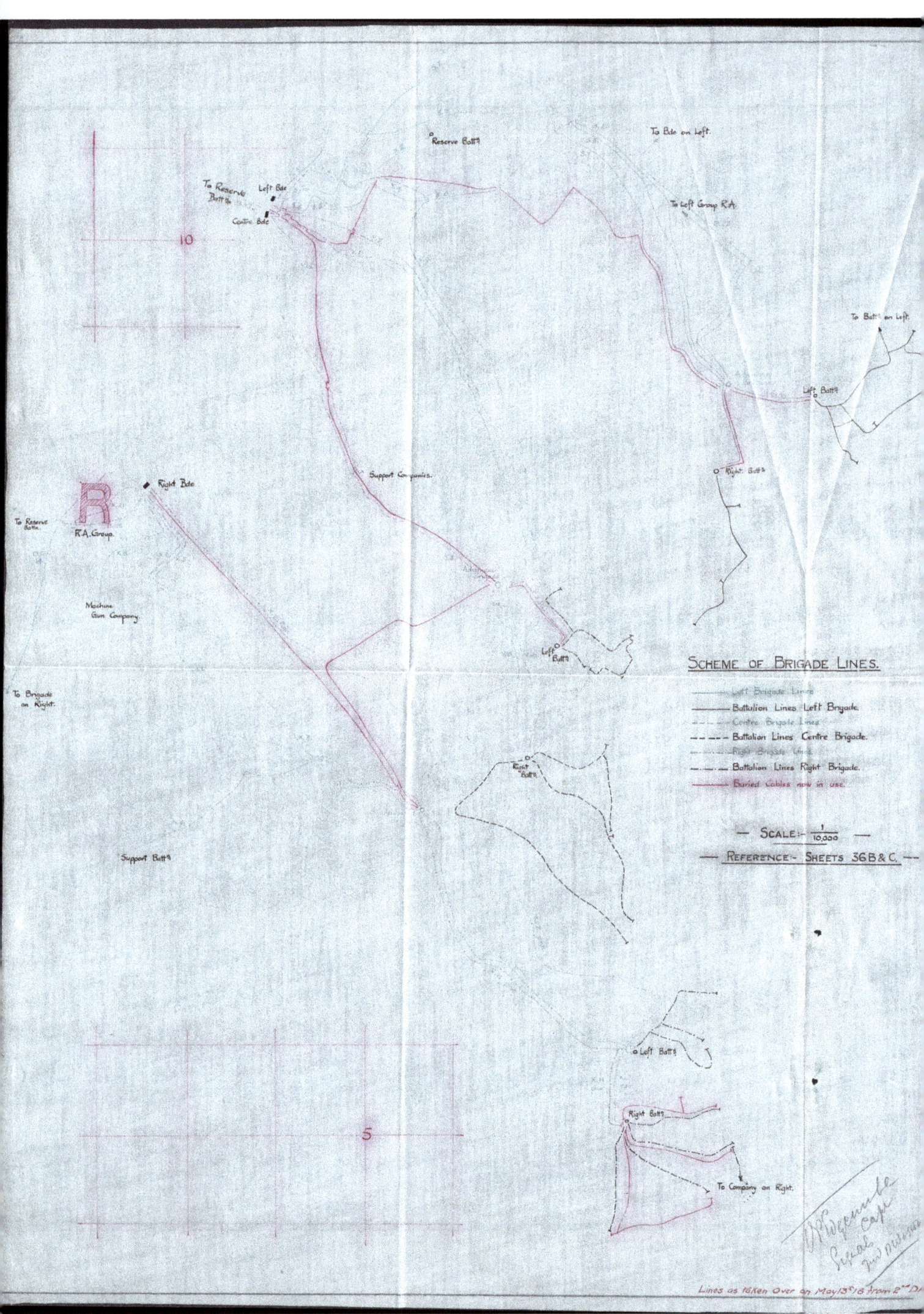

Sigmund Coy 23 D
16.6.7.

Army Form C. 2118.

WAR DIARY
or
INTELLIGENCE SUMMARY.

(Erase heading not required.)

CONFIDENTIAL

War Diary
of
23rd Divl. Signal Coy R.E.
for
June 1916

Jaster
Maj. R.E.
OC. 23rd Sig. C.R.E.
1/7/16

WAR DIARY
INTELLIGENCE SUMMARY.
(Erase heading not required.)

Army Form C. 2118.

Place	Date	Hour	Summary of Events and Information	Remarks and references to Appendices
SAINS-en-GOHELLE	1 June		Holding NOULETTE Sector; N°2 Sec at AIX; N°4 Sec at BULLY; N°3 Sec at HERSIN; N°1 Sec (ex Capt Operators.Inniseen) at BARLIN. Operating & Maintenance; Erecting 8-line Circuit; 2nd	M
Do	2 June		Visual party of 12 men joined → Operating & Maintenance. Erecting 8-line Circuit	M
Do	3 June		Operating and Maintenance. Completed first 8-line circuit to YWR.	M
Do	4 June		Operating and Maintenance. Started 5th line and 4 line circuits from BOYEFFLES & Co.	M
Do	5 June		Operating and Maintenance. Sapper Randles awarded Military Medal	M
Do	6 June		Operating and Maintenance. Circuit active continued	M
Do	7 June		Operating and Maintenance. Circuit active continued	M
Do	8 June		Operating and Maintenance. Picked up unused R.A. lines in Notre Dame de LORETTE C.T. road	M
Do	9 June		Operating and Maintenance. 69 Bty Visual Class completed instruction	M
Do	10 June		Operating and Maintenance. Started last portion of 8-line circuit. BOYEFFLES & YWR. N°2 Sec to HERSIN; N°3 Sec to AIX-NOULETTE.	M

WAR DIARY
or
INTELLIGENCE SUMMARY.
(Erase heading not required.)

Army Form C. 2118.

Place	Date	Hour	Summary of Events and Information	Remarks and references to Appendices
SAINS-en-GOHELLE	11 June		Operating & Maintenance	JM
Do	12 June		Operating & Maintenance	JM
Do	13 June		Operating & Maintenance. Completed last 8-line circuit and handed over New Scheme of lines as well as old Scheme taken over from 2nd Div.	JM
BRUAY	14 June		Relieved by 47.5 Div. and marched from SAINS, BARLIN & BRUAY. Signal-time put on 1 hour at 11 p.m.	JM See plans A and B
Do	15 June		Operating & Maintenance.	JM
BOMY	16 June		Marched to BOMY & went into billets at PETIGNY.	JM Sea-plan C
Do	17 June		Operating & Maintenance.	JM
Do	18 June		Operating & Maintenance	JM
Do	19 June		Tactical Exercise with 2 brigades to practice assault and aeroplane signalling. Operating & Maintenance.	JM
Do	20 June		Operating & Maintenance. All Divisional Visual Stations sent to Bdes to remain and work Visual to Div.	JM

WAR DIARY
or
INTELLIGENCE SUMMARY.
(Erase heading not required.)

Army Form C. 2118.

Instructions regarding War Diaries and Intelligence Summaries are contained in F. S. Regs., Part II. and the Staff Manual respectively. Title pages will be prepared in manuscript.

Place	Date	Hour	Summary of Events and Information	Remarks and references to Appendices
BOMY	21 June		Operating & Maintenance.	M
BOMY	22 June		Skeleton tactical exercise for signalling with aeroplanes.	M
do	23 June		Operating & Maintenance. Eighth Buzzer-class temporarily suspended for move.	M
	24 June	3.0 p.m.	Marched to BERGUETTE.	M
		9.40 a.m.	Left BERGUETTE by train.	
		4.40 p.m.	Arrived AMIENS and marched to VAUX-en-AMIENOIS. Advance party put through from St-SAUVEUR	M
VAUX	25 June		Operating & Maintenance. Put through lines from St-SAUVEUR exchange to St-PIERRE, TIRAN-COURT & BELLOY.	M See plan D
do	26 June		Operating & Maintenance.	M
do	27 June		Operating & Maintenance	M
do	28 June		Took over a pair from 17th Div. from ALLONVILLE to COISY; laid from POULAINVILLE via COISY to MOLLIENS-au-BOIS. Marched to ALLONVILLE in order to open there at 8.30 p.m.; orders cancelled.	M
do	29 June		Laid a pair from BERTANGLES to VAUX owing to Div HQ remaining there while Div was moved.	M
do	30 June		Party returned from ALLONVILLE to make room for 68th B.de.	M See plan E

SECRET.

SUBSIDIARY MEANS OF SIGNALLING.

VISUAL: *Handed over to 47th Divn June 14th 1916.*

The following visual stations are manned and worked day and night with signals in both directions :-

    Right Brigade Advanced   (P.A.) - R.29.d.2.8.
    Left Brigade Advanced   (P.B.) - R.24.a.5.3.
    Transmitting Station   (N.L.) - R.34.d.0.3.
    Divisional H.Q.   (Y.W.) - R. 8.a.0.6.

The means employed are :-

    between Y.W. and N.L., helio, lamp and large flag;
    between N.L. and P.A., lamp, small flag and flapper;
    between N.L. and P.B., helio, lamp and large flag.

There are 1 N.C.O. and 16 men employed exclusively on this work.

WIRELESS:

The following stations are working :-

(1) Z.T., close to right battalion headquarters in SOUCHEZ Section (Map Square S.1.b.1.5); works to Z.F.

(2) Z.F., on NOTRE DAME de LORETTE (Map Square X.4.b.4.9.); works to Z.C.

(3) Z.C., at Divisional Headquarters. - R.1.d.7.3.

PIGEONS:

98 birds are kept at the Brasserie in SAINS-EN-GOHELLE (R.2.c.4.7) (R.2.c.7.5) and at the Farm opposite (R.2.c.4.7.)   These birds are for both NOULETTE and CARENCY Sectors.   As regards NOULETTE Sector only 4 birds are sent to Left Bde. daily and 4 to Right Bde.

Three N.C.Os. and men are employed exclusively on Pigeon Service.

The following are also required :-

Two cycle orderlies at the lofts to take messages to the Signal Office when the birds arrive.

Four trained men to receive the birds at the headquarters of brigades, take them to Battn. headquarters and deal with messages; two men at the headquarters of each Bde. in the line.

Circuit Diagram
26.6.16

BCO

Y.W. ← Vaux-en Amienois

G
Q

Sig Subt

24th Bde St Sauveur

68th Bde Tirapcourt

RA Belloy

A 68 Bde St Pierre

Gurler
Maj. R.E.
26/6/16

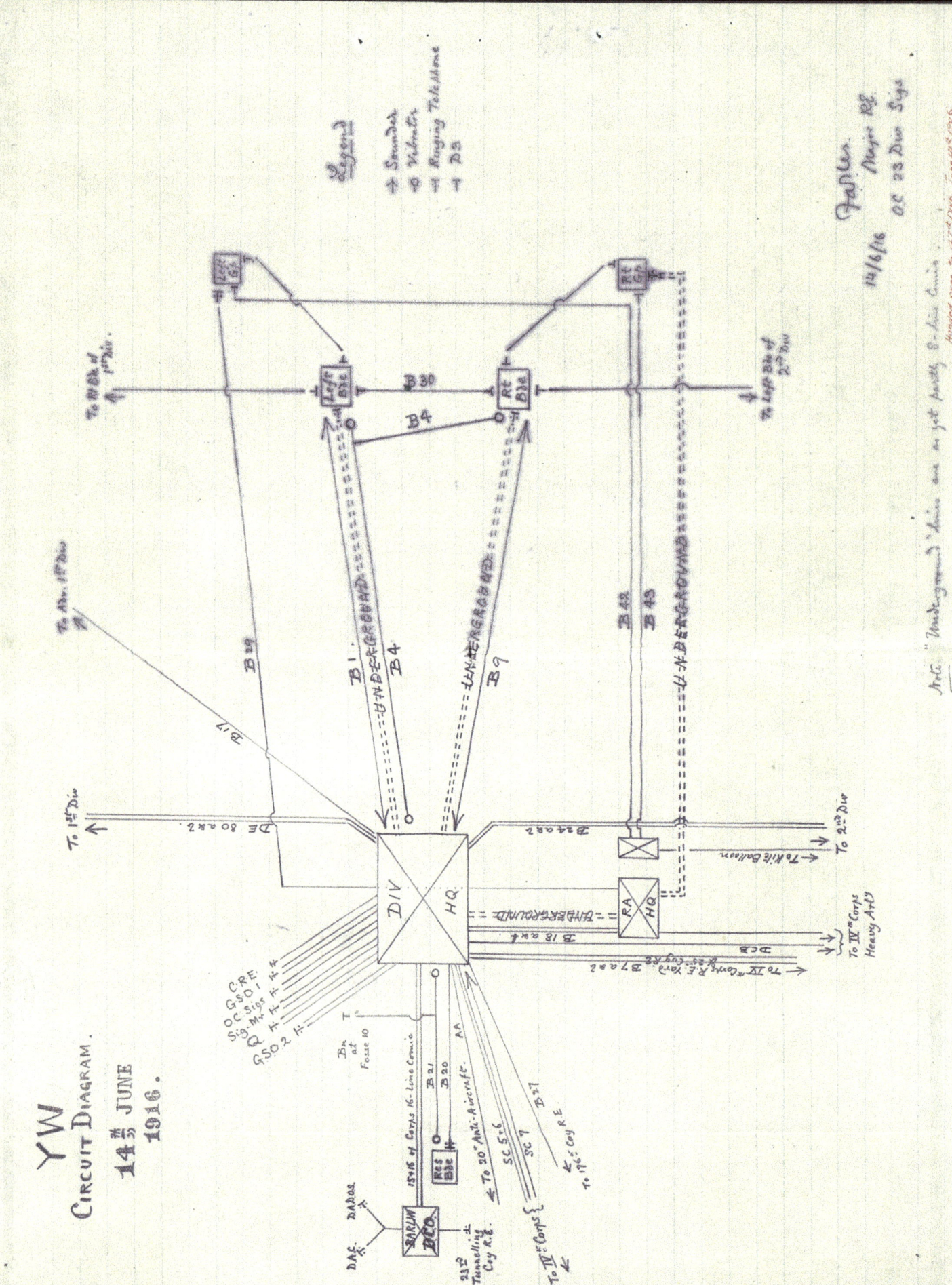

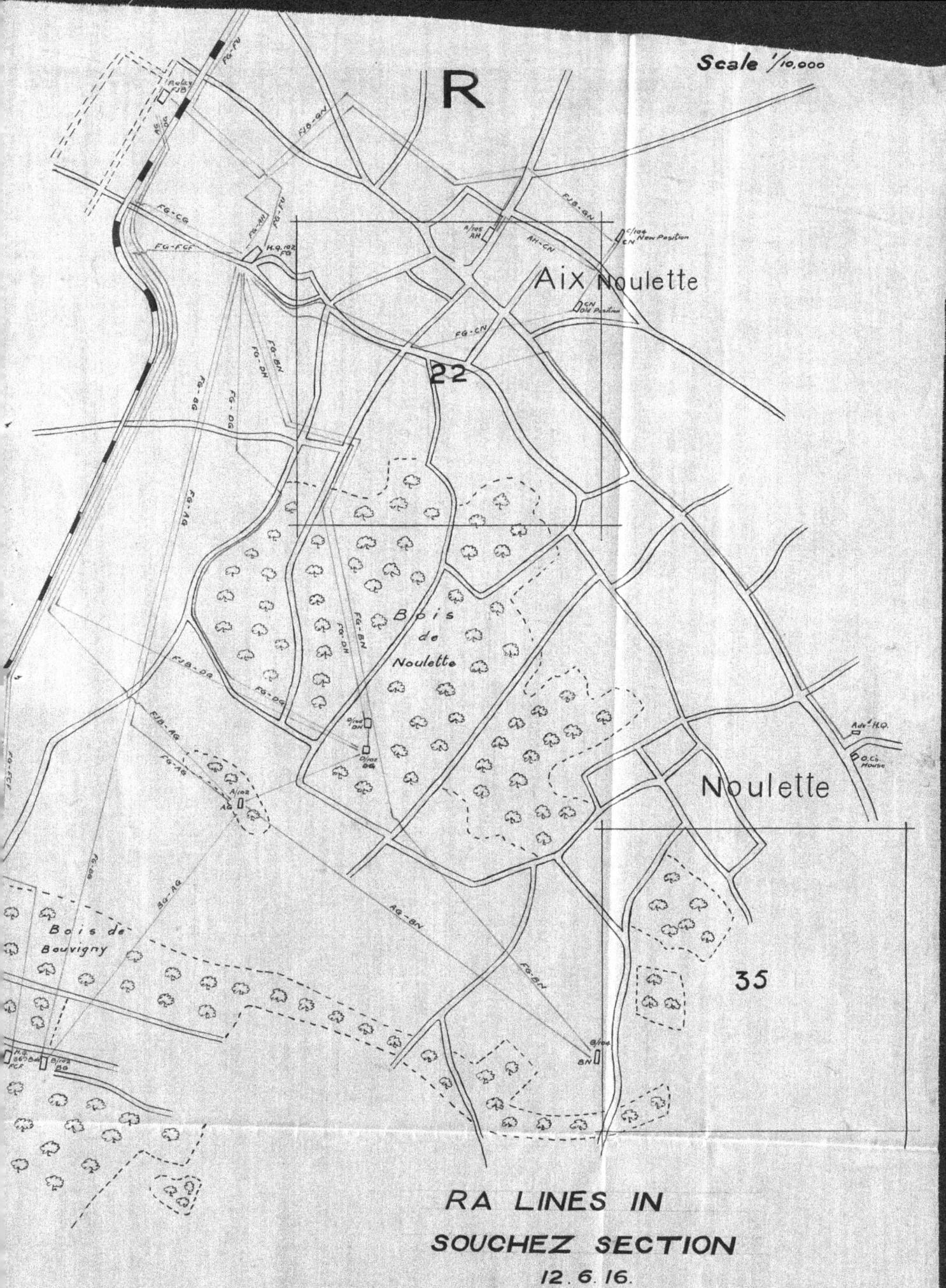

SHEWING DIVISIONAL TELEPHONE GRAPH LINES

REF SHEETS: 56D&C SCALE: 1/10000

Advanced Div. on Left.

- 6
- 2 — 3
- H.Q. Div.
- Res. Batt. L. Bde.
- Left Group R.A.
- H.Q. Left Bde.
- 12
- 8 — 9
- M.G. Coy.
- R.A.
- 15 — 16
- Right Bde. H.Q.
- Right Group R.A.
- 24 — 19
- 21 — 22
- Res. Batt. R. Bde.
- R
- 30 — 25
- 27 — 28
- To Brigade on Right.
- 33 — 34
- Div. O.P.

TRACING SHEWING DIVISIONAL TELEPHONE AND TELEGRAPH LINES

Ref Sheets 36 B & C Scale: 1/10,000

176th Coy R.E.
M.M.G. Batt

5 Reserve Bde	6		2	3
			HQ Div	
			Res. Batt. L. Bde.	
11	12		8 M.G. Coy	9

COMIC · AIRLINES ·
CABLE · LINES ·

R.A.

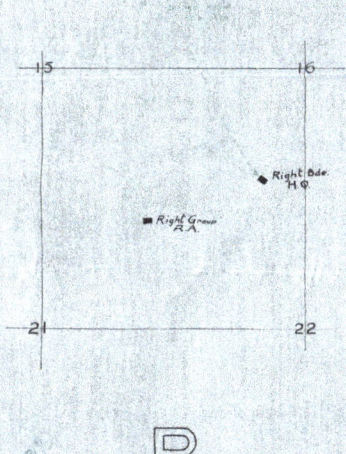

15 — 16
Right Bde H.Q.
Right Group R.A.
21 — 22

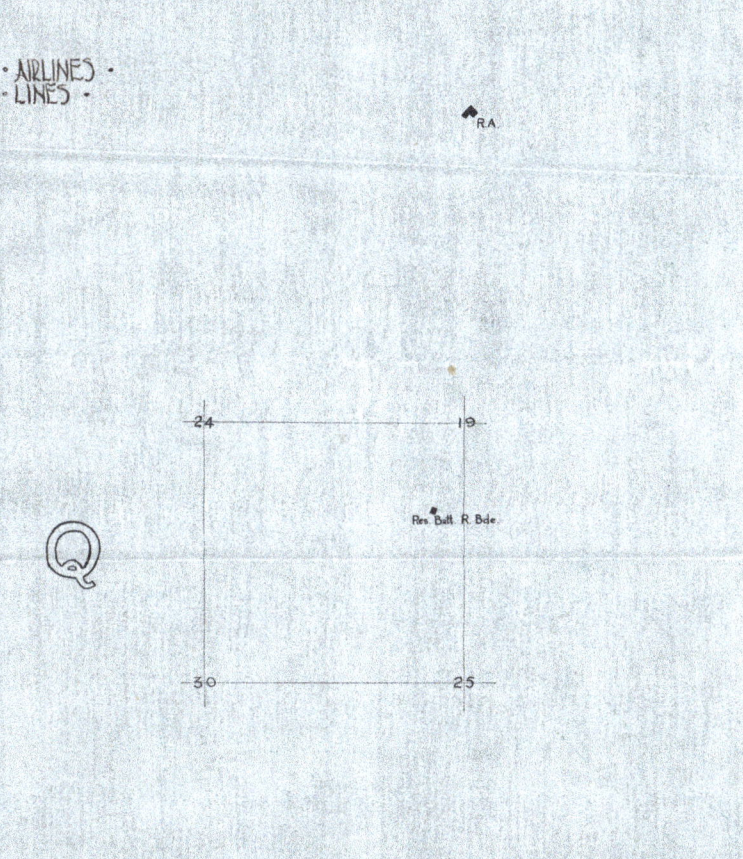

24 — 19
Res. Batt. R. Bde.

Q

30 — 25

R

27 — 28
To Brigade on Right
33 — 34

Divl O.P.

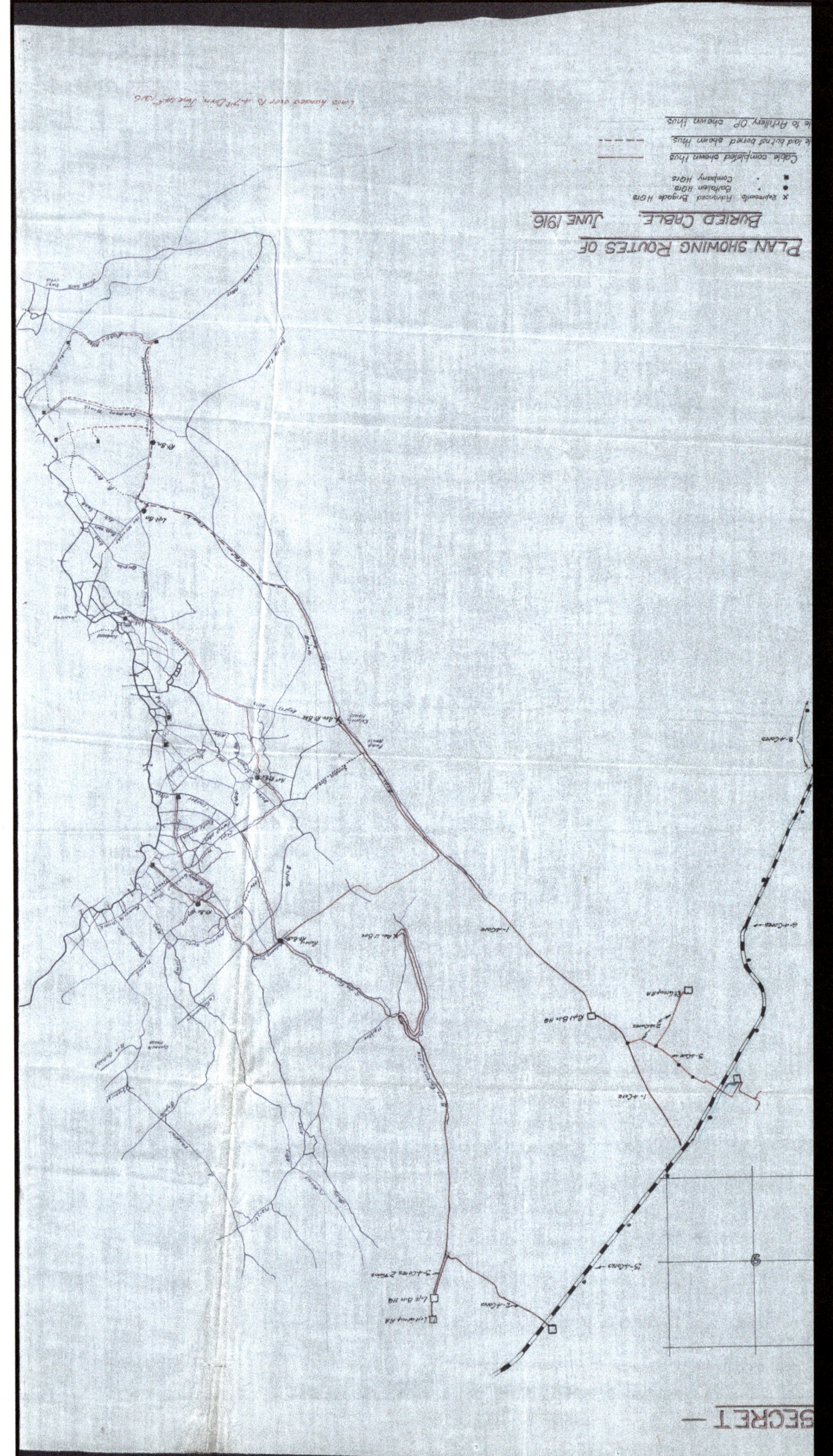

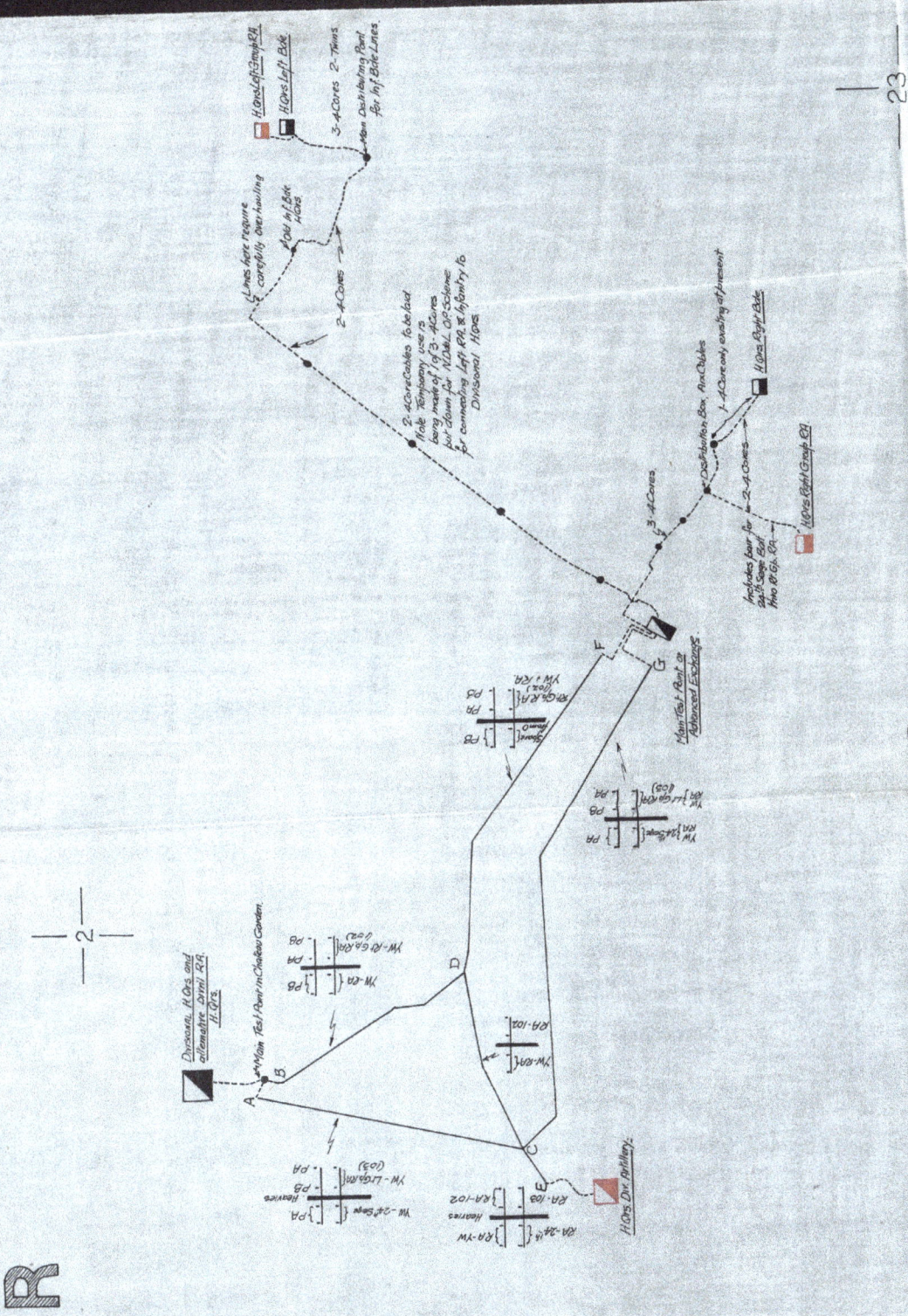

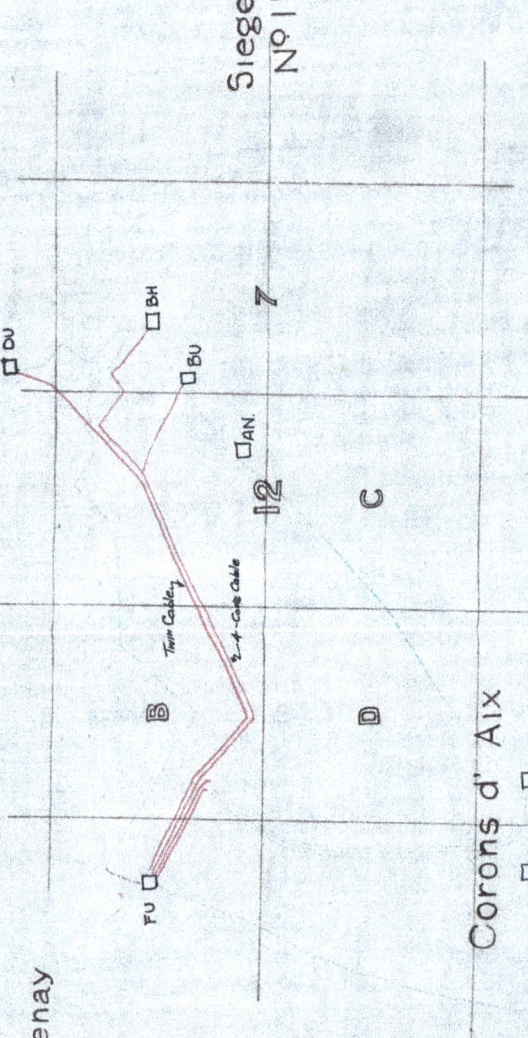

SCHEME OF BRIGADE LINES.

- - - - Battalion Lines Right Brigade.
―――― Buried Cables
―――― Proposed Buried Cables

SCALE :- 1/10,000

REFERENCE :- SHEETS 36 B & C.

Major RE
O.C. 23rd Divl. Signal Coy.
Royal Engineers

Lines handed over to 47th Divn June 4th 1916.

CIRCUIT DIAGRAM
14/6/16

68th Bde, CRÉPY
24th Bde, DIÉVAL
69th Bde DIVION

D.R.
D.R.

G Q

To Naval Div.
To IVth Corps
To BRUAY Civil Exchange

Gates.
Major R.E.
O.C. 23rd Div. Sig. Co. R.E.

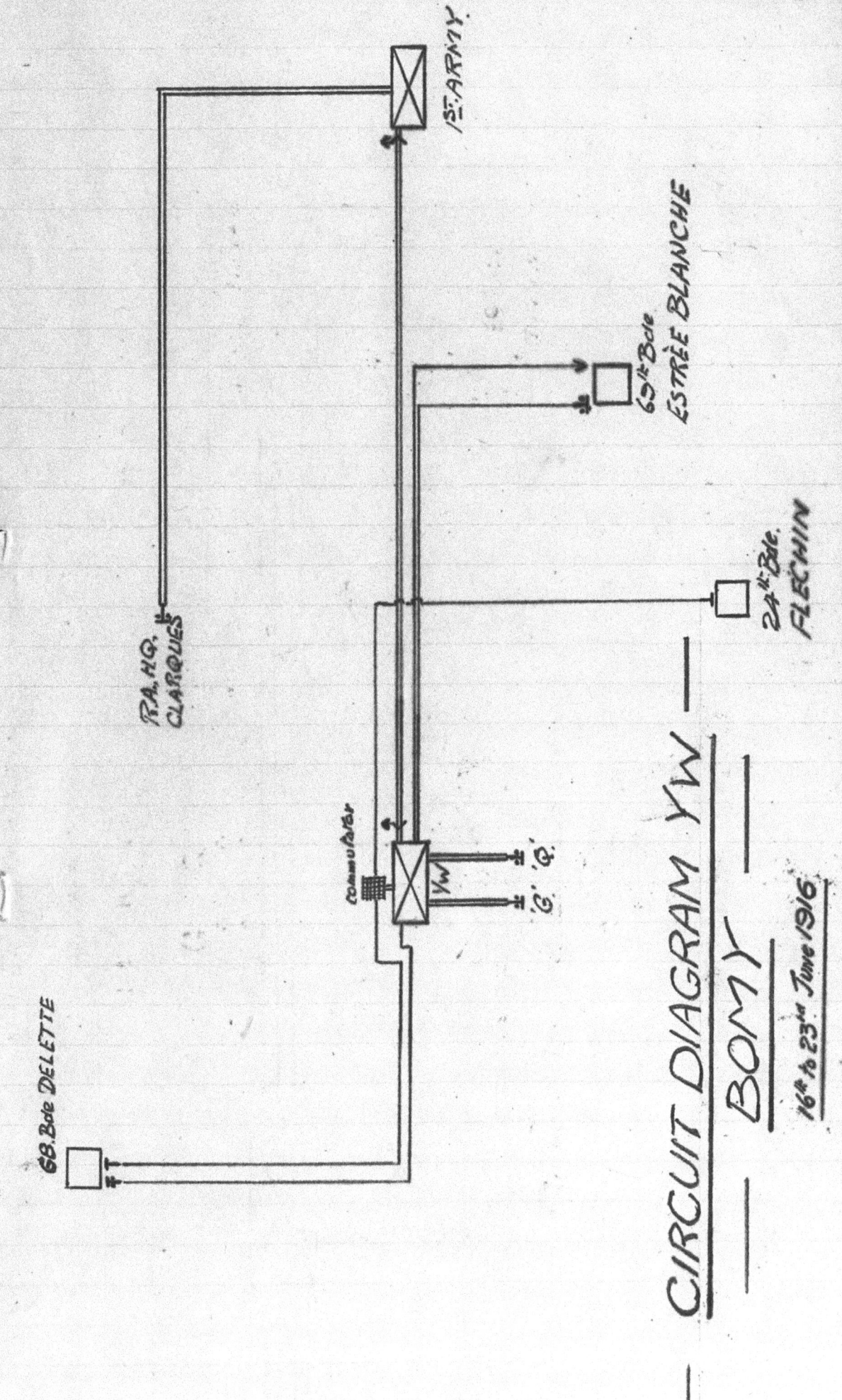

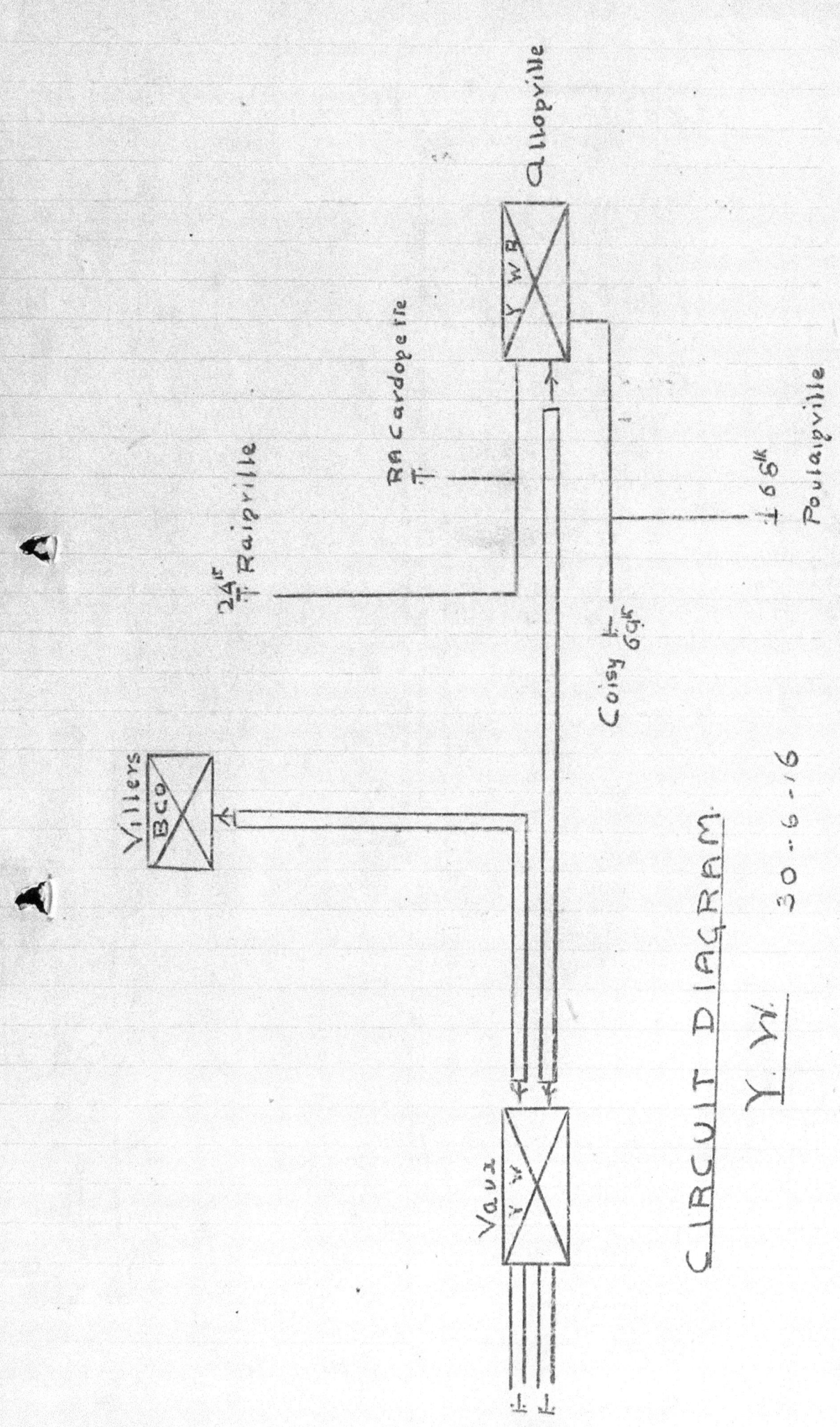

23/2

July.

Army Form C. 2118.

23 Div Sig nals

Vol 8

WAR DIARY

~~INTELLIGENCE SUMMARY~~

(Erase heading not required.)

Summary of Events and Information

WAR DIARY
of
23rd Div. Signal Coy R.E.
1st–31st July 1916.

James.
Maj. RE.
9/8/16

Army Form C. 2118.

WAR DIARY
or
INTELLIGENCE SUMMARY.
(Erase heading not required.)

Instructions regarding War Diaries and Intelligence Summaries are contained in F.S. Regs., Part II. and the Staff Manual respectively. Title pages will be prepared in manuscript.

Place	Date	Hour	Summary of Events and Information	Remarks and references to Appendices
VAUX-en-AMIENOIS	July 1		In II nd Corps, V th (Reserve) Army. Marched at 8.0 p.m., relieving up from VAUX to BERTANGLES.	IM
BAIZIEUX	July 2		Took over HQ office of 12th Div., joined III rd Corps, Fourth Army.	IM See plan A
Do	July 3		By means of existing lines, cable got 68th & 69th Bdes. which moved up from FRANVILLERS and BAIZIEUX to MILLENCOURT and ALBERT respectively.	IM
MOULIN du VIVIER	July 4		Marched to MOULIN du VIVIER and relieved 34th Div. in the line	IM
Do	July 5		23rd Div R.A. ordered into action between FRICOURT & BÉCOURT wood at 5 p.m. Laid 4 lines to 4 R.A. Bdes. at 6.0 p.m. (14 miles of cable) and guns went into position at dark. Also put through one old underground line station overhead line from MOULIN du VIVIER to BÉCOURT Châu South.	IM See plan B
Do	July 6		Took over Forward Exchange to Bde lines from 17 th Div. owing to side-step South.	IM Do C
Do	July 7		Put through old overhead line to BÉCOURT Châu.	IM
Do	July 8		Re-laid lines behind HQ of RA bdes; laid cable from F. Exch. to Visual Sta. S. of FRICOURT	IM
Do	July 9		Laid 1 mile of G.I. armoured Smd. from YWR to 69th Bde HQ at SCOTS REDOUBT, and continued to D 5 to point 56, preparing to attack on CONTALMAISON.	Fd.l
Do	July 10		Capture of Contalmaison; v. plan F.	Fd.l

Army Form C. 2118.

WAR DIARY
or
INTELLIGENCE SUMMARY.
(Erase heading not required.)

Instructions regarding War Diaries and Intelligence Summaries are contained in F.S. Regs., Part II. and the Staff Manual respectively. Title pages will be prepared in manuscript.

Place	Date	Hour	Summary of Events and Information	Remarks and references to Appendices
St GRATIEN	11 July		Relieved by 1st Div. and moved out to rest, leaving D Dets at MOULIN DU VIVIER for R.A. Communications	OM
Do	12 July			M
Do	13 July			M
Do	14 July			M
Do	15 July		No 4 (Bde) section arrived from POULAINVILLE after departure of 24th Bde to rejoin 8th Div and pending arrival of 70th Bde to rejoin 23rd Div	OM
Do	16 July			M
Do	17 July		No 4 (Bde) Sec. to 70th Bde at PIERREGOT.	M
Do	18 July		C Dets to MOULIN DU VIVIER to assist D owing to increasing length of R.A. lines.	M
Do	19 July			M
Do	20 July			M
HÉNENCOURT MOLLIENS	21 July		Started moving into line again. Reeled up from PIERREGOT to St GRATIEN and tee from	OM

2353 Wt. W2544/1454 700,000 5/15 D.D.&L. A.D.S.S./Forms/C. 2118.

WAR DIARY
or
INTELLIGENCE SUMMARY.

Army Form C. 2118.

Place	Date	Hour	Summary of Events and Information	Remarks and references to Appendices
HÉNENCOURT	22 July			Day
Do	23 July			Day
Do	24 July			Day
Do	25 July		Sent parties to ALBERT to put through CM 3·4 from BLACK WOOD and 4 line comic from F⁹ Exch. at BÉCOURT Ch⁴ to ALBERT and cable through the streets to Div HQ.	Day
ALBERT	26 July		Relieved 1st Div in the line. Out with HQ at Rue de NEMOURS, ALBERT until of MOULIN du VIVIER joined HQ at ALBERT. Detachments from MOULIN du VIVIER.	Day See plan D
Do	27 July			Day
Do	28 July		Poling Trunk Nº 2 and R.A. lines. Reel'd up YA 3.	Day
Do	29 July		Div HQ moved out of the town on the MILLENCOURT road, W27 c 6·7.	Day
Do	30 July		Started 8-line comic from BLACK WOOD to BELLEVUE Farm and 12-line comic from SOULT Bridge to new HQ; VII Corps assisting by putting up the portion from BELLEVUE Farm to SOULT Bridge.	Day
Do	31 July		Finished Airline (8 and 12 lines) from BLACK WOOD to new HQ at W27 c 6·7 and opened Signal Office there at 8.0 pm under canvas.	Day See plan E

CIRCUIT DIAGRAM
YW
2.7.16

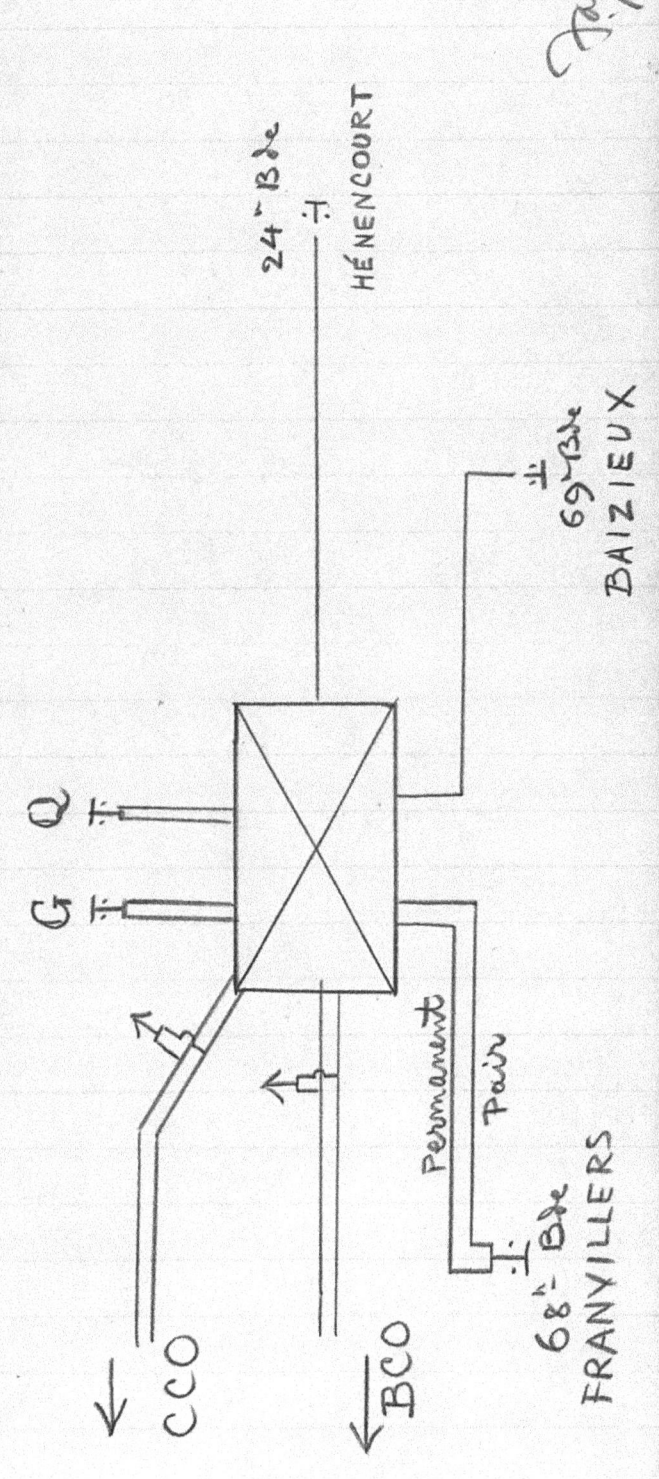

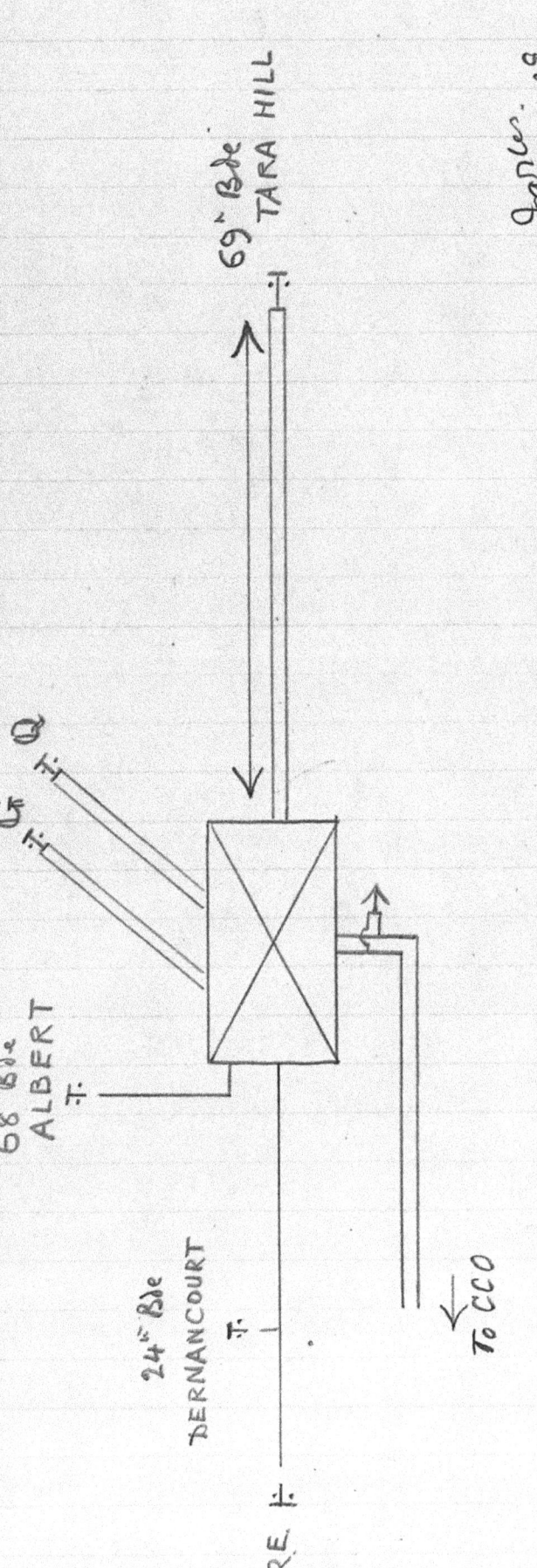

C

CIRCUIT DIAGRAM
YW
Forward Lines
6.7.16

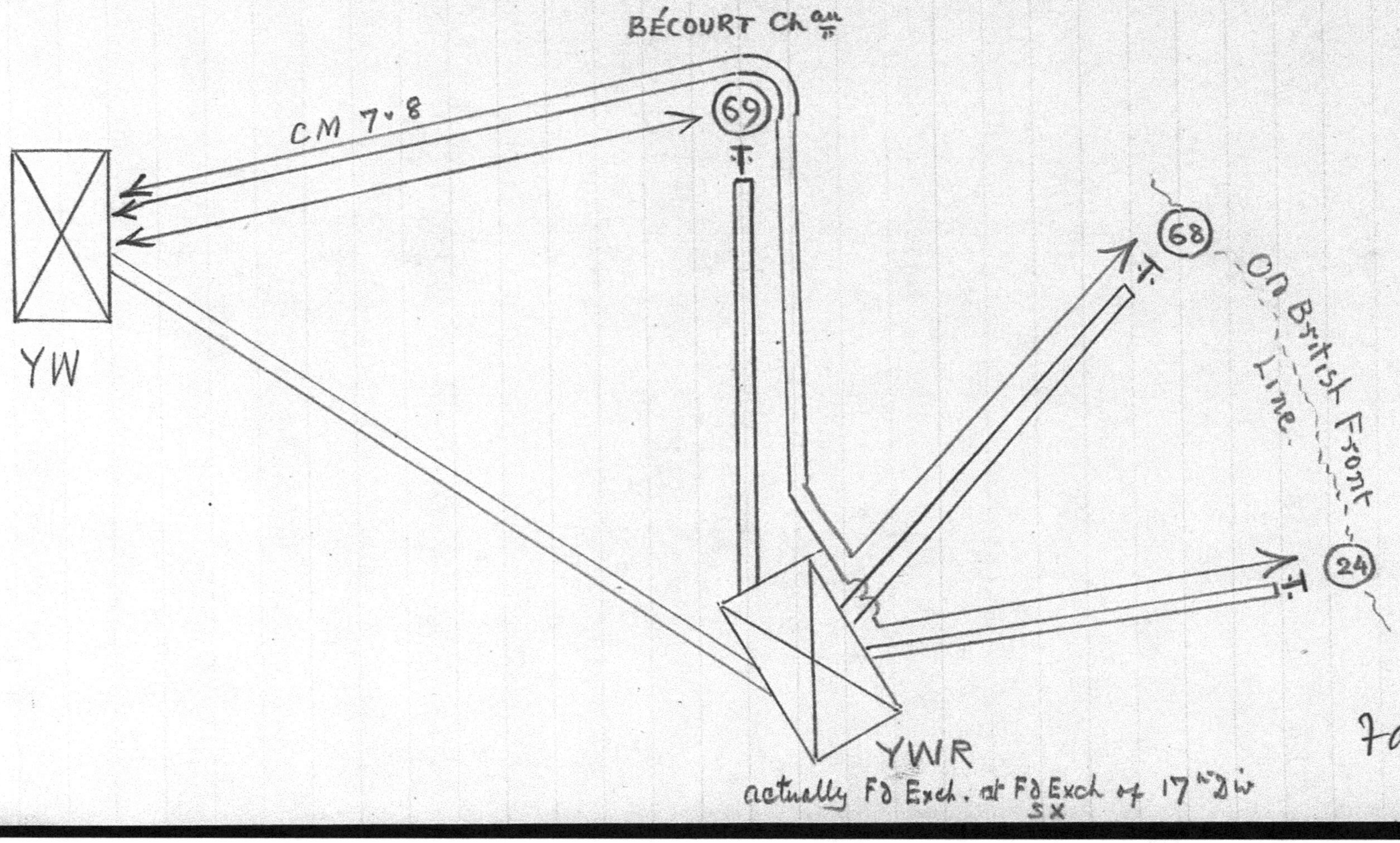

On British Front Line

(24) T.

(68) T.

BÉCOURT Ch̄ āu

(69) T.

CM 7·8

YWR
actually Fd Exch. at Fd Exch. of 17th Div
SX

Fuller
Maj. R.S.

YM

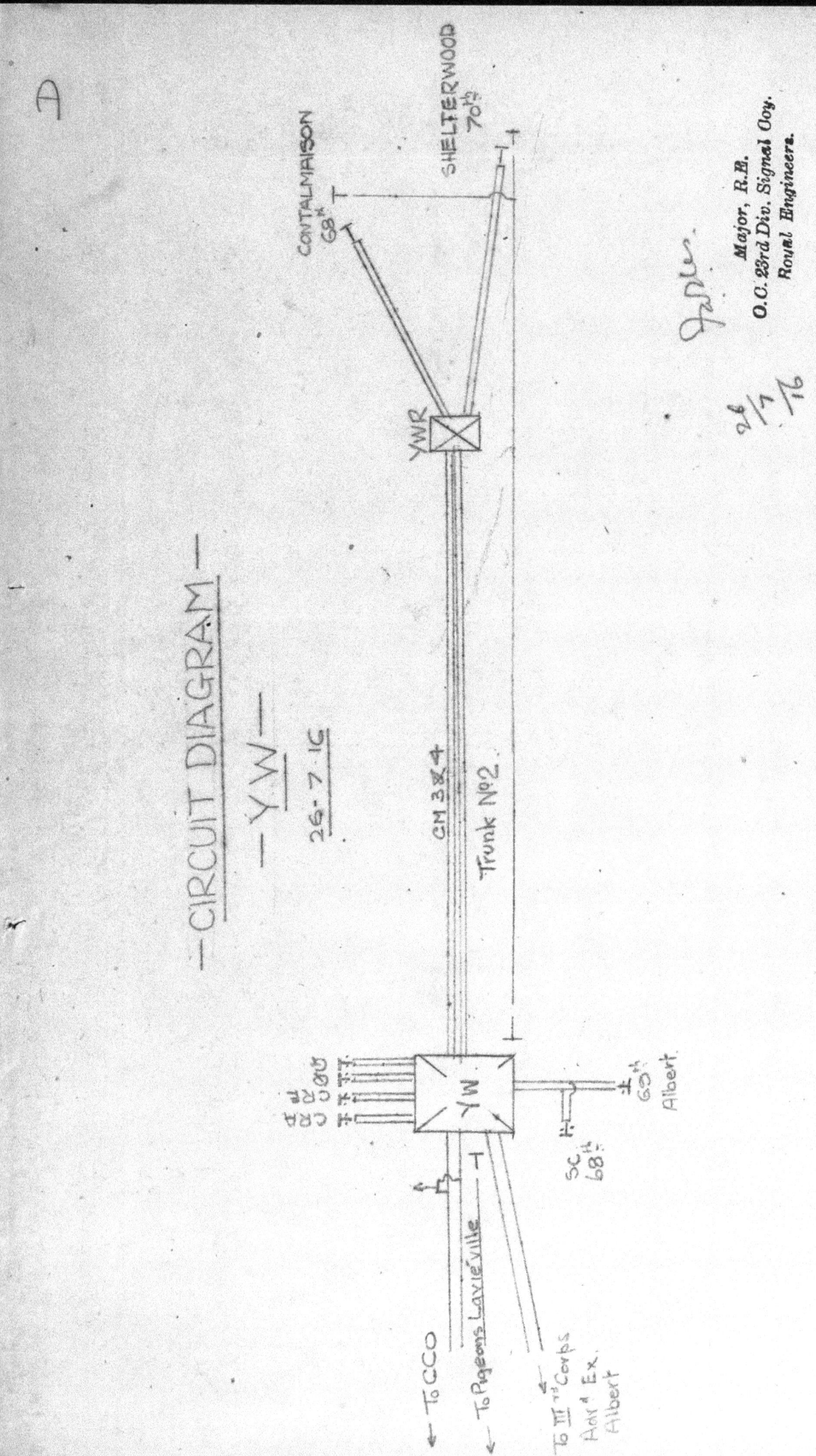

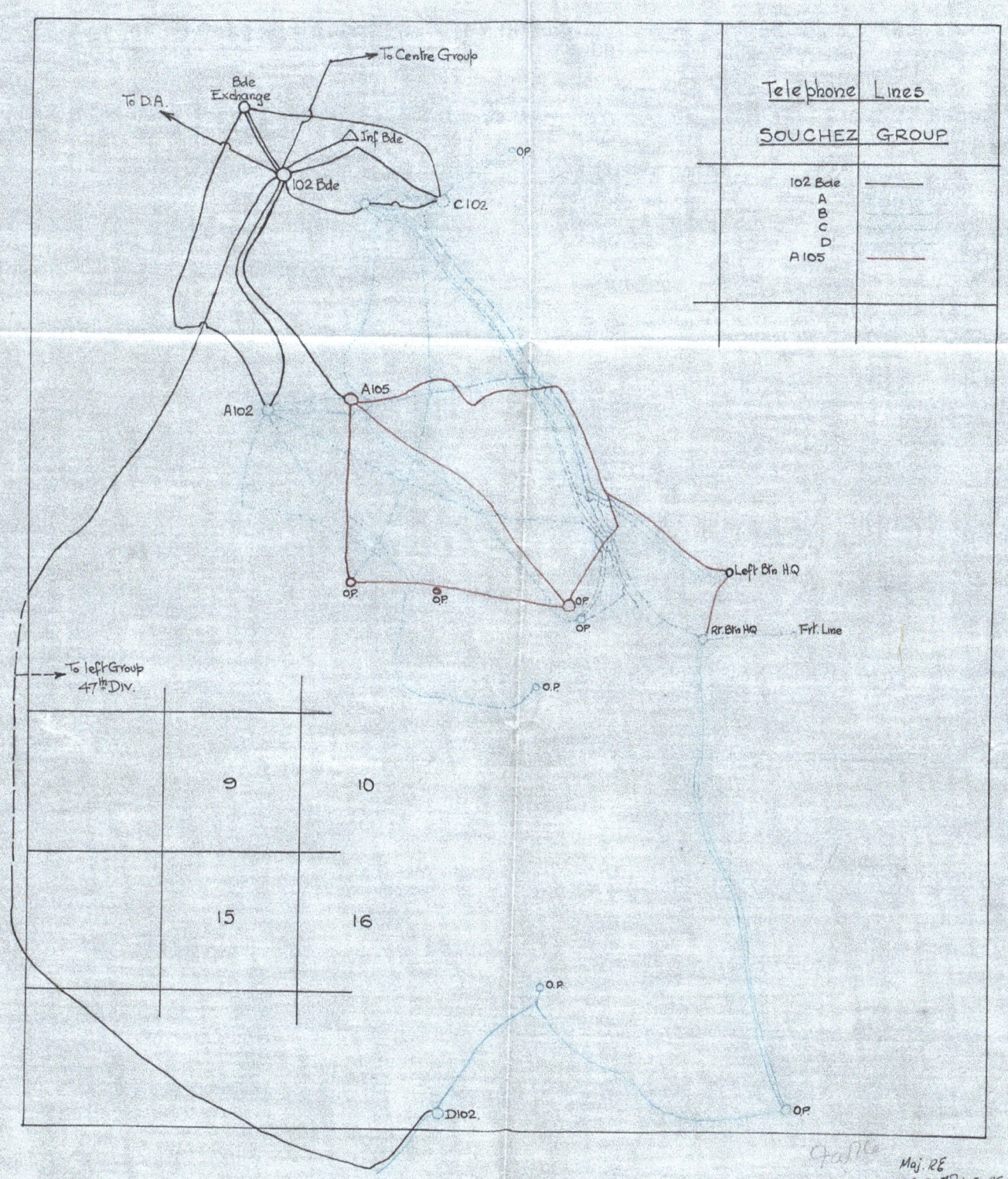

23rd Divisional Engineers

23rd DIVISIONAL SIGNAL COMPANY R. E.

AUGUST 1 9 1 6

Army Form C. 2118.

WAR DIARY
or
~~INTELLIGENCE SUMMARY.~~

(Erase heading not required.)

Signals

Vol 9

WAR DIARY
of
23rd Signal Coy R.E.

1st – 31st August 1916

Jasker.
Major R.E.
31/8/16

WAR DIARY
or
INTELLIGENCE SUMMARY.

(Erase heading not required.)

Army Form C. 2118.

Place	Date	Hour	Summary of Events and Information	Remarks and references to Appendices
ALBERT	Aug 1st		Forming part of III rd Corps, Fourth Army, operating on the SOMME; Brigade Headquarters in the line at SHELTER WOOD and CONTALMAISON	9 M
do	Aug 2nd		Completed line from SHELTER WOOD to CONTALMAISON by armoured cable.	9 M
do	Aug 3rd		Opened a station for aeroplane to drop messages N. of BÉCOURT WOOD. Started a comic fair from BELLEVUE Farm Direct to R.A. advanced H.Q. at FRICOURT.	A M
do	Aug 4th		Continued R.A. Comic fair and completed it.	P M
do	Aug 5th		Started R.A. Artillery (4 line)	9 M
do	Aug 6th		Continued R.A. Artillery	9 M
do	Aug 7th		Finished R.A. Artillery to FRICOURT.	9 M
BAIZIEUX	Aug 8th		Handed over to 15th Division advanced to BAIZIEUX, leaving Divl Artillery still in the line and 1 officer & 20 other ranks to carry on signals.	9 M
do	Aug 9th		Resting.	9 M
do	Aug 10th		Mounted portion marched to POULAINVILLE at 2.0 pm en route for AILLY-LE-HAUT-CLOCHER	A M
AILLY-LE-HAUT CLOCHER	Aug 11th		Dismounted portion trained from FRÉCHENCOURT to LONGPRÉ for AILLY-LE-HAUT-CLOCHER to join X th Corps	A M

Army Form C. 2118.

WAR DIARY
or
INTELLIGENCE SUMMARY.
(Erase heading not required.)

Instructions regarding War Diaries and Intelligence Summaries are contained in F. S. Regs., Part II. and the Staff Manual respectively. Title pages will be prepared in manuscript.

Place	Date	Hour	Summary of Events and Information	Remarks and references to Appendices
AILLY-LE-HAUT-CLOCHER	Aug. 12ᵗʰ		Resting.	pm
FLÊTRE	Aug. 13ᵗʰ		Marched to LONGPRÉ at 4.45am and entrained. Arrived at BAILLEUL at 6.40 p.m. and marched to FLÊTRE, joining IXᵗʰ Corps, Second Army.	pm
FLÊTRE	Aug. 14ᵗʰ		} Resting.	
Do	Aug. 15ᵗʰ		}	pm
Do	Aug. 16ᵗʰ		}	
STEENWERCK	Aug. 17ᵗʰ		Marched at 9.0 a.m. to NIEPPE and took over huts and bare lines of 41ᵗʰ Signal Co. Took over lines & offices of 41ˢᵗ Division at STEENWERCK at 6.0 p.m. Brigades at PONT DE NIEPPE (68), BRUNE-GAYE (70ᵗʰ) and ROMARIN (69ᵗʰ). Operating & Maintenance.	pm
Do	Aug. 18ᵗʰ		Operating & Maintenance.	pm
Do	Aug. 19ᵗʰ		Operating & Maintenance.	pm
Do	Aug. 20ᵗʰ		Operating & Maintenance.	am
Do	Aug. 21ˢᵗ		Operating & Maintenance.	pm

WAR DIARY
or
INTELLIGENCE SUMMARY.

(Erase heading not required.)

Army Form C. 2118.

Place	Date	Hour	Summary of Events and Information	Remarks and references to Appendices
STEENWERCK	Aug 22nd	—	Operating & Maintenance	App 1
do	Aug 23rd	—	Operating & Maintenance	App 1
do	Aug 24th	—	Operating & Maintenance	App 1
do	Aug 25th	—	Laid cable from railway crossing on BAILLEUL-STEENWERCK road to 70th Bde. Road School at A 2 c but through a railway to crossing S. of NIEPPE thence by spare wires pair to YPER	App 1
do	Aug 26th	—	Erecting open wire pair from 70th HQ at BRUNE-GAYE to Res. Bn at PONT-DE-NIEPPE.	App 1
do	Aug 27th	—	Laying armoured cable S.O.S. lines in deprecate necessitated by regrouping	App 1
do	Aug 28th	—	Operating & Maintenance	App 1
BAILLEUL	Aug 29th	—	Div HQ moved to BAILLEUL at 11.0 a.m. making room for the 51st Div HQ moving back from AR-MENTIÈRES.	App 1
do	Aug 30th	—	Wiring offices.	App 1
do	Aug 31st	—	Operating & Maintenance	App 1

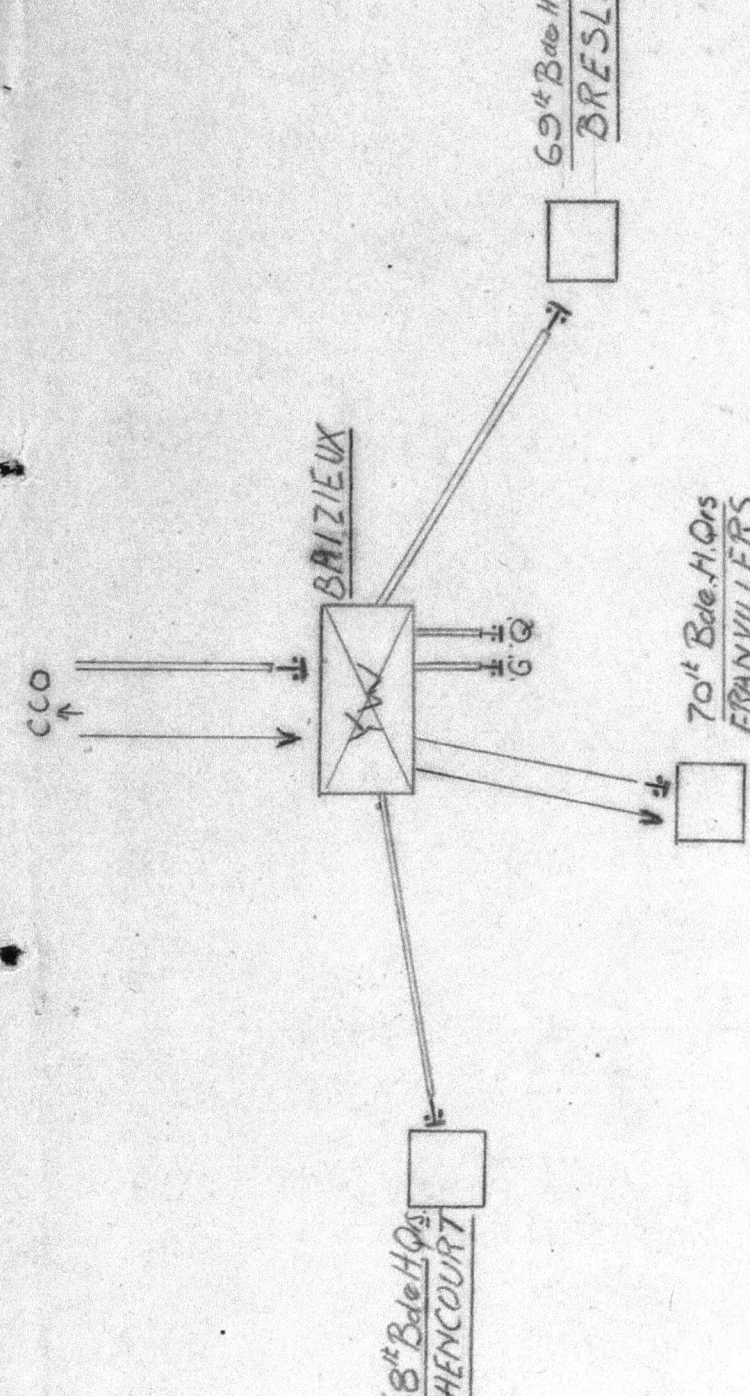

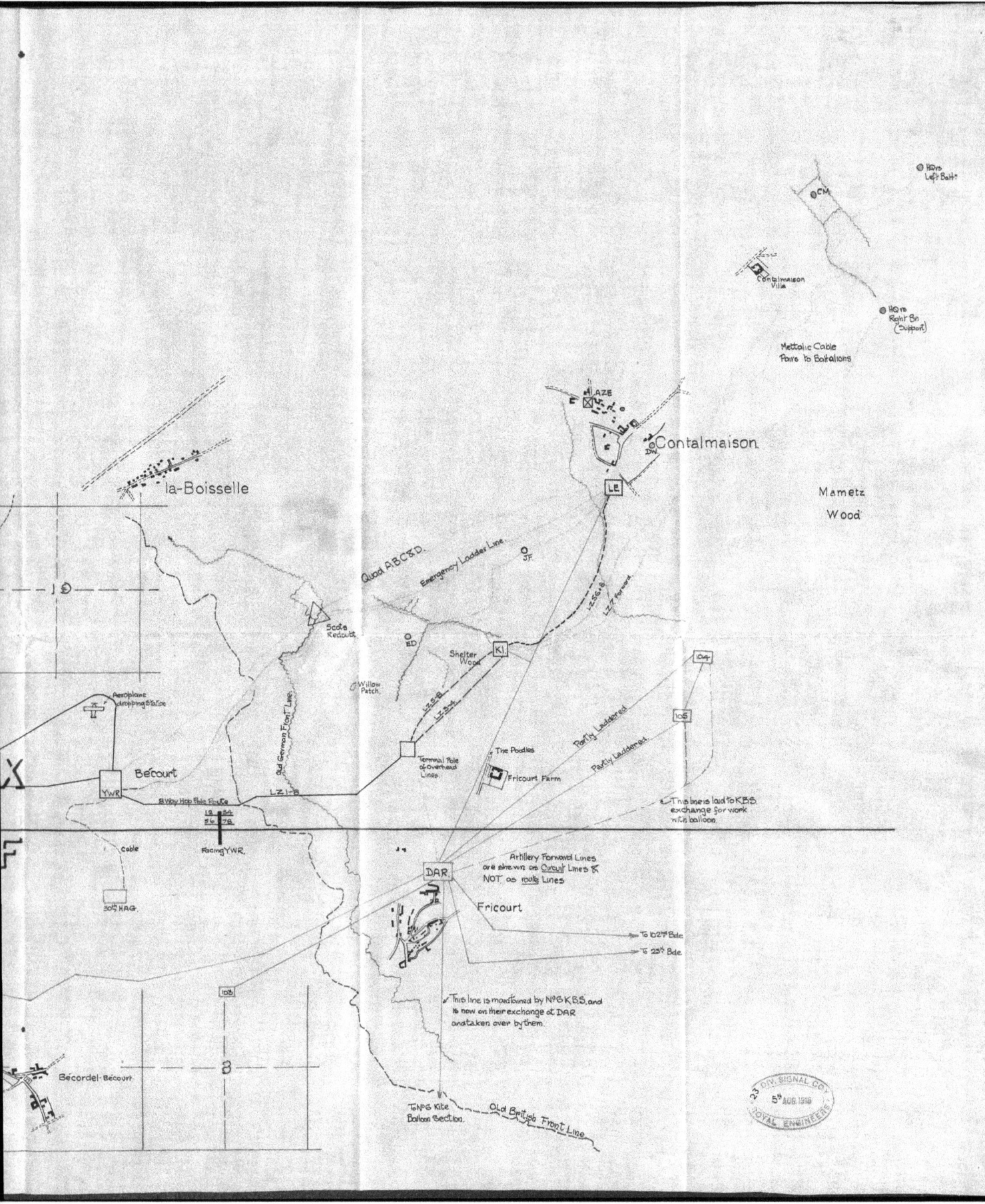

YW COMMUNICATIONS.

— AUGUST 5TH '16. —

— SCALE :- 1/10,000. —

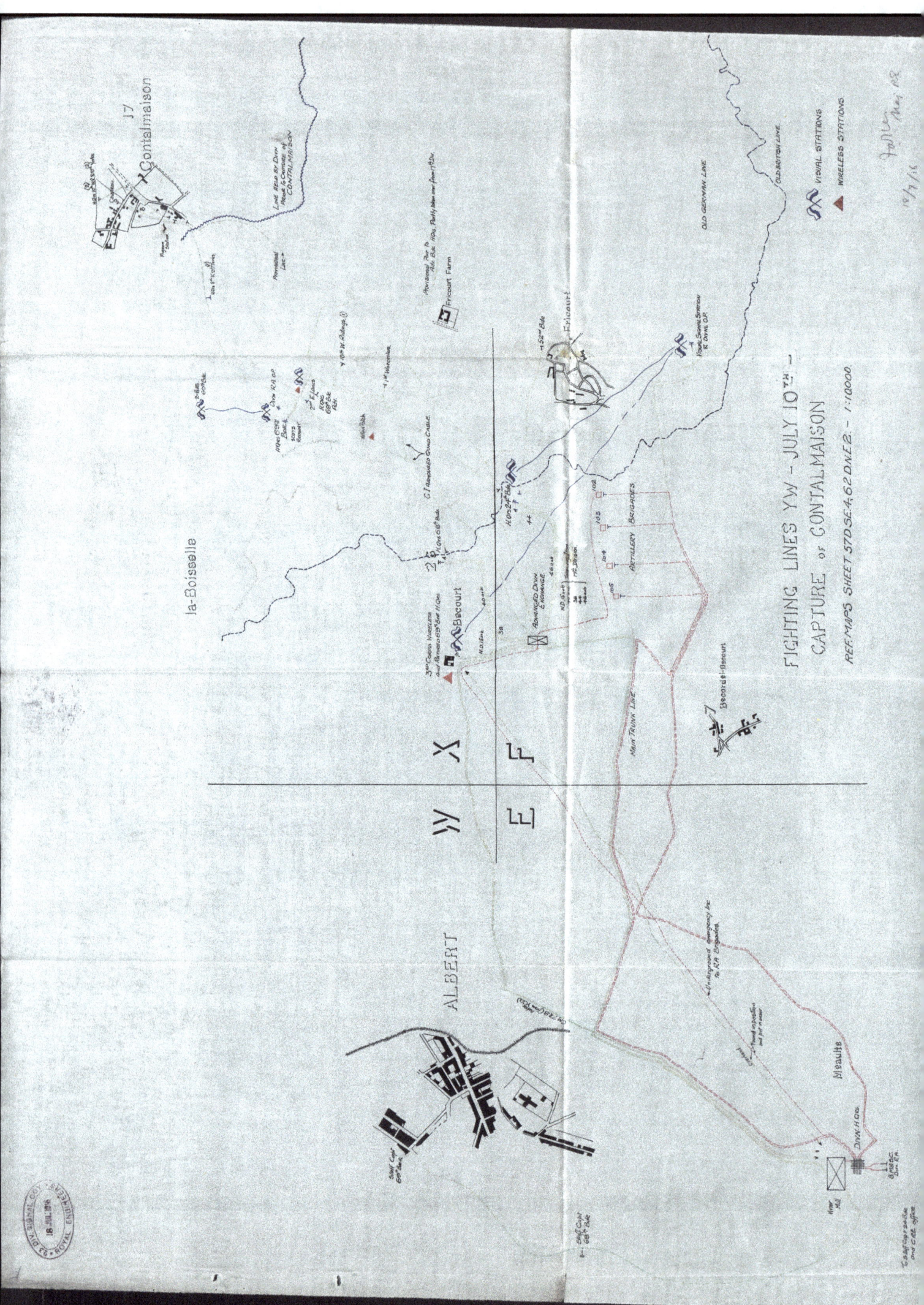

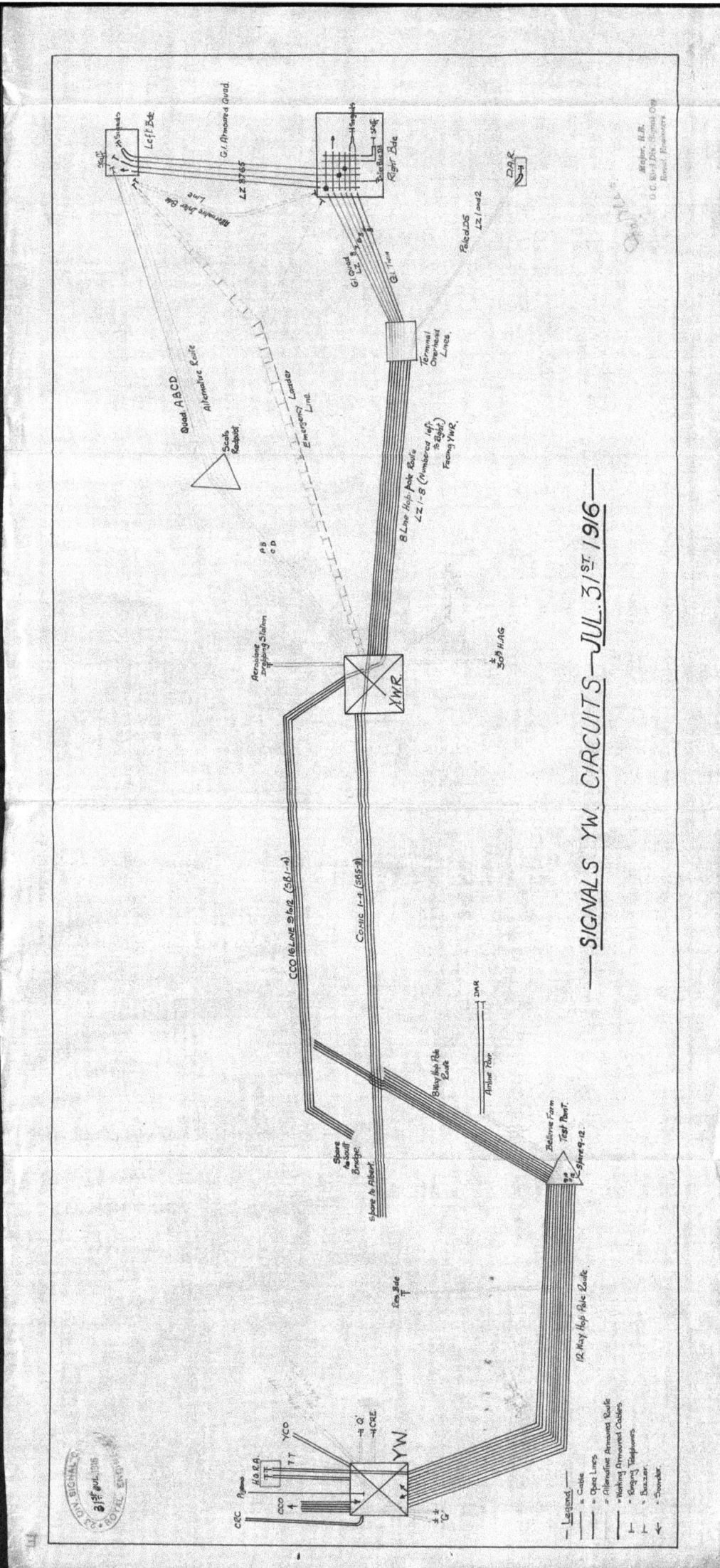

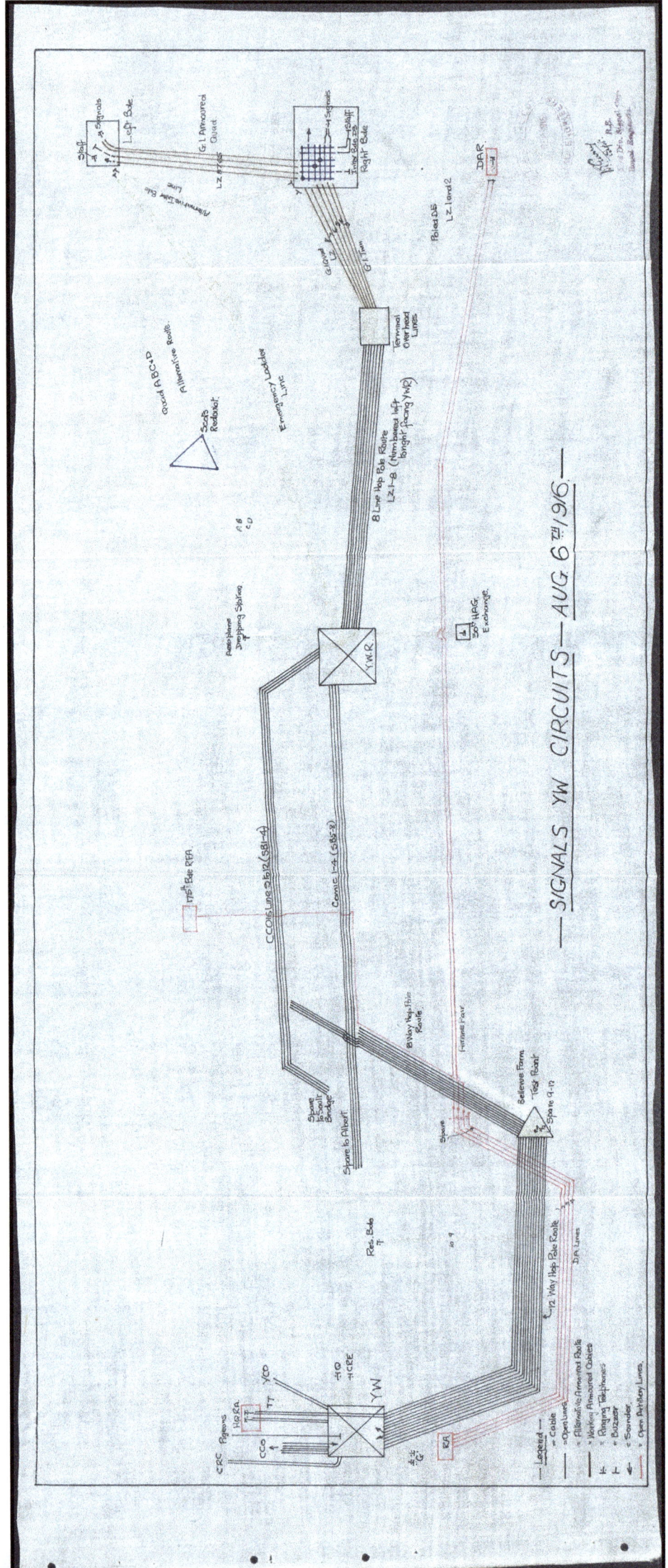

WAR DIARY

OF

23RD SIGNAL COY., R.E.

1st – 30th September 1916

WAR DIARY
or
INTELLIGENCE SUMMARY.
(Erase heading not required.)

Army Form C. 2118.

Instructions regarding War Diaries and Intelligence Summaries are contained in F.S. Regs., Part II. and the Staff Manual respectively. Title pages will be prepared in manuscript.

Place	Date	Hour	Summary of Events and Information	Remarks and references to Appendices
BAILLEUL	Sept. 1st		Main I.G. the R.F. joined 2nd Army Signals. Shooting and reconnaissance	
"	Sept. 2nd		Shooting and reconnaissance	
"	Sept. 3rd		do	
"	Sept. 4th		do	
"	Sept. 5th		3 humber personnel marched to Tilques. Reserve parks proceeded to TILQUES	
TILQUES	Sept. 6th		Closed at BAILLEUL 10am opened at TILQUES same time	
"	Sept. 7th		Coy. continued march to TILQUES. Remainder arrived by train at 2pm. Captain J.A. TILLARD R.E. joined & assumed the Coy. 2/Lt Tanson & Taylor joined Coy. as Supernumerary	
"	Sept. 8th		Shooting and reconnaissance	
"	Sept. 9th		do	
"	Sept. 10th		Reserve parks by Coy to AMIENS to prepare offices at BALLONVILLE	
ALLONVILLE	Sept. 10th		Coy entraining at ST OMER - detrained at LONGEAU & march to ALLONVILLE. D.R.s and lorries proceeded by road. Opened at 10pm.	
"	Sept. 11th		Lines laid K 69 1/2 Brigade & COISY	
BAZIEUX	Sept. 12th		Coy marched to BAZIEUX Closed Office at ALLONVILLE 9.30 am opened at BAZIEUX same time	

WAR DIARY
or
INTELLIGENCE SUMMARY.
(Erase heading not required.)

Army Form C. 2118.

Place	Date	Hour	Summary of Events and Information	Remarks and references to Appendices
BAIZIEUX	Sept. 13th		Operating and maintenance	⟵
"	Sept. 14th		do	⟵
"	Sept. 15th		do	Standing by to move at 2 hours notice	⟵
"	Sept. 16th		do	⟵
"	Sept. 17th		do	⟵
"	Sept. 18th		Moved advance party to HQrs Horse ALBERT & relieve 15th Div. Sgl.	⟵
MILLENCOURT–ALBERT Road	Sept. 19th		Moved by to ALBERT. Closed office at 10am opened at new HQrs same time.	⟵
"	Sept. 20th		Partis working on R.A. lines. Testing and maintenance. Continued buried lines MARTINPUICH.	⟵
"	Sept. 21st		Forward Exchange taken up. Start extension to future buried run, continued	⟵
"	Sept. 22nd		Buried cable towards MARTINPUICH. Work on forward lines and Buried Cable.	⟵
"	Sept. 23		Work on Forward lines, R.A. lines and buried cables (see diagram)	⟵

WAR DIARY
or
INTELLIGENCE SUMMARY.
(Erase heading not required.)

Army Form C. 2118.

Place	Date	Hour	Summary of Events and Information	Remarks and references to Appendices
ALBERT	Sept. 24th		Work on Brick Road and trench rond Shelter Wood. Trenches sent to SHELTER & MALA WOOD.	
	Sept. 25		Work on R.A. Lines and Bronca Road.	
	Sept. 26		Operating and Reconnaissance — do —	
	Sept. 27th		— do —	
	Sept. 28th		Work on Bronca Lines and R.A. Lines.	
	Sept. 29th		Laid down 1" MARTIN PUICH from end of tram to Brigade moving up.	
	Sept. 30th		Preparation for attack and move of Hqrs. 1 SHELTER WOOD next day.	

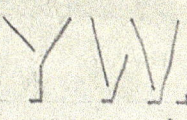

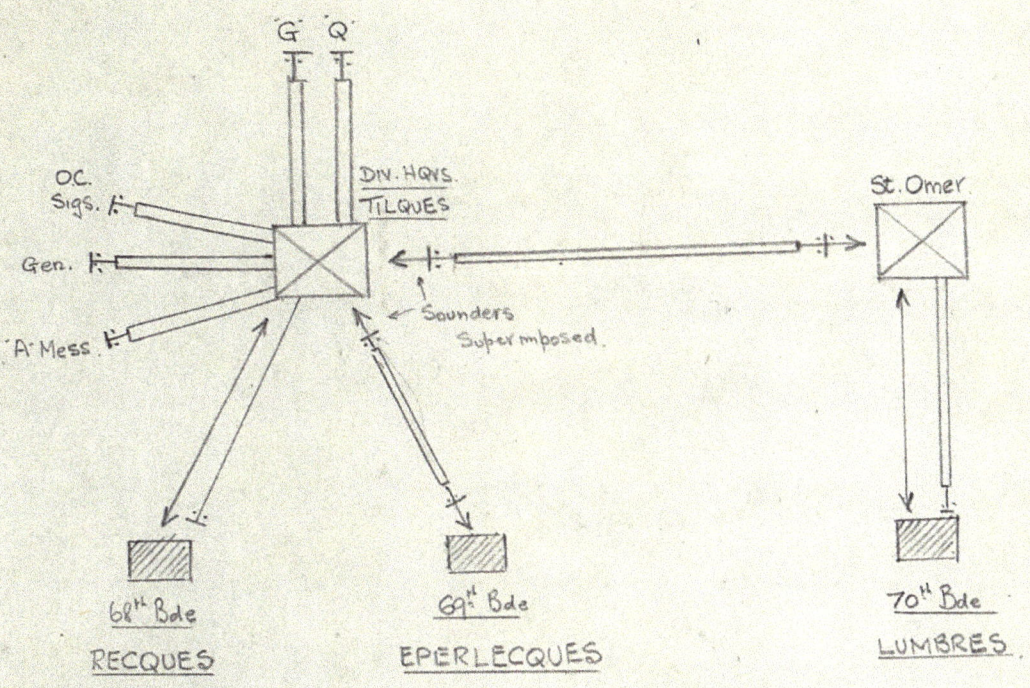

CIRCUIT DIAGRAM - TILQUES -
— 6-9-16 —

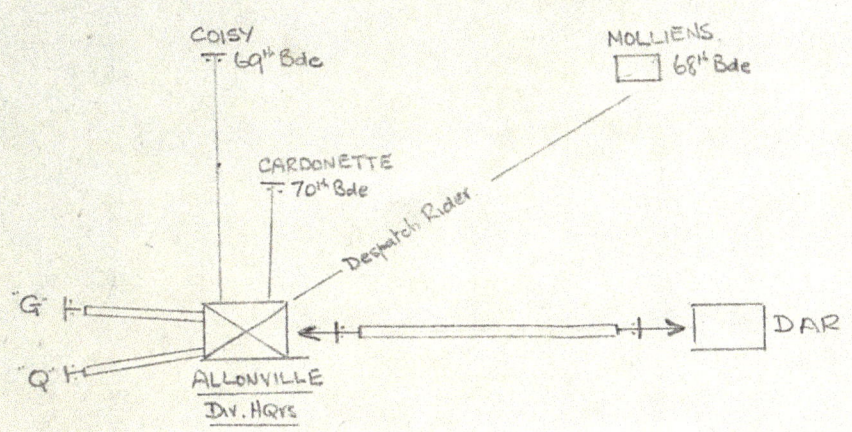

— CIRCUIT DIAGRAM - ALLONVILLE —
— 10·9·16 —

Legend

Ringing 'Phones thus —:|

Sounders "   →

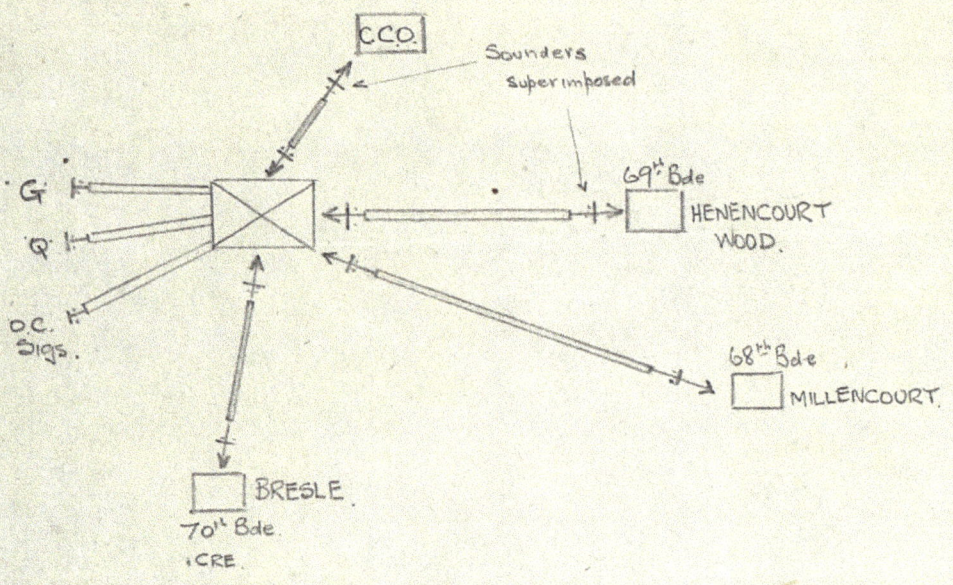

CIRCUIT DIAGRAM — BAIZIEUX

12-9-16

Legend

Ringing 'Phones thus ——|

Sounders · ——→

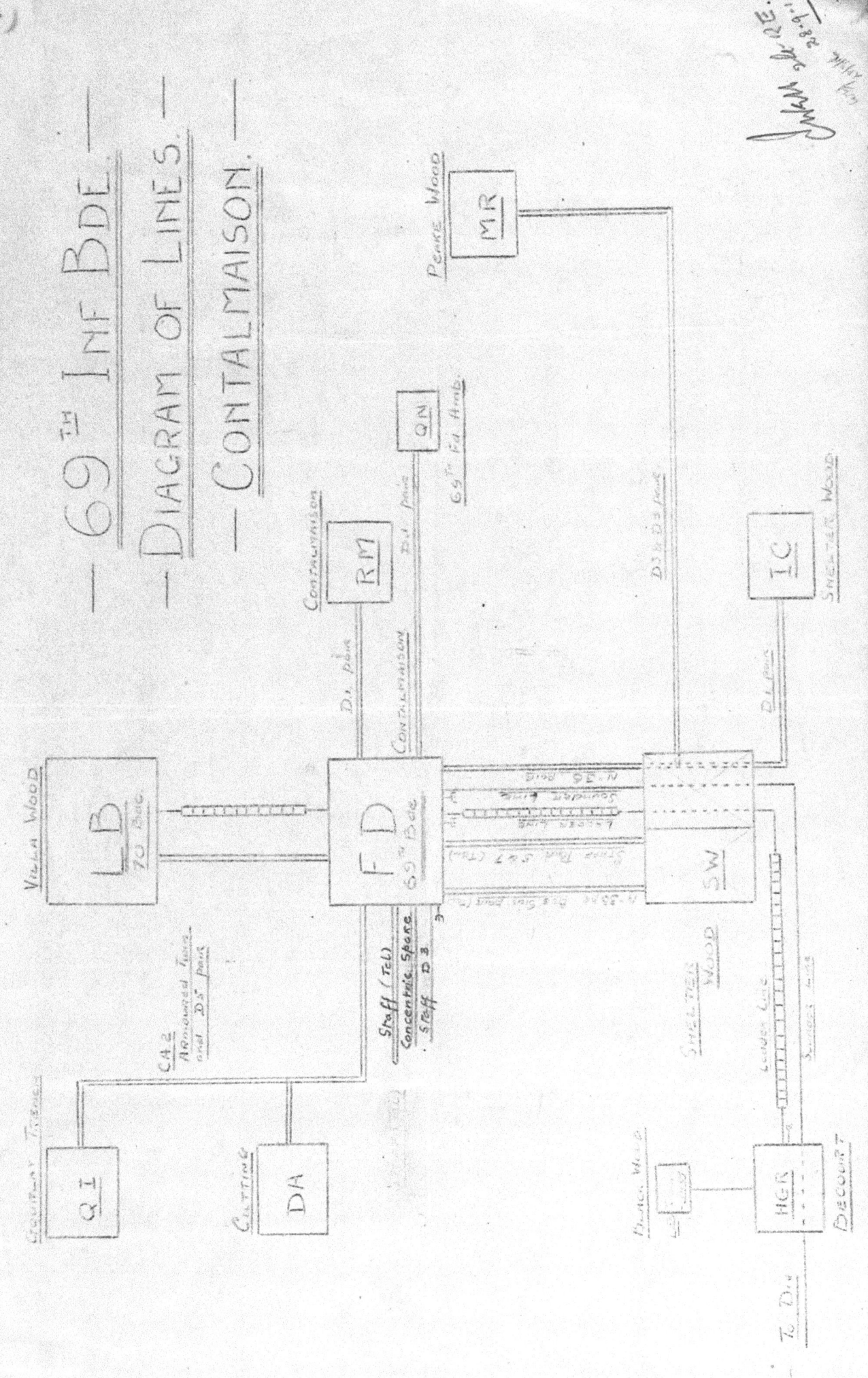

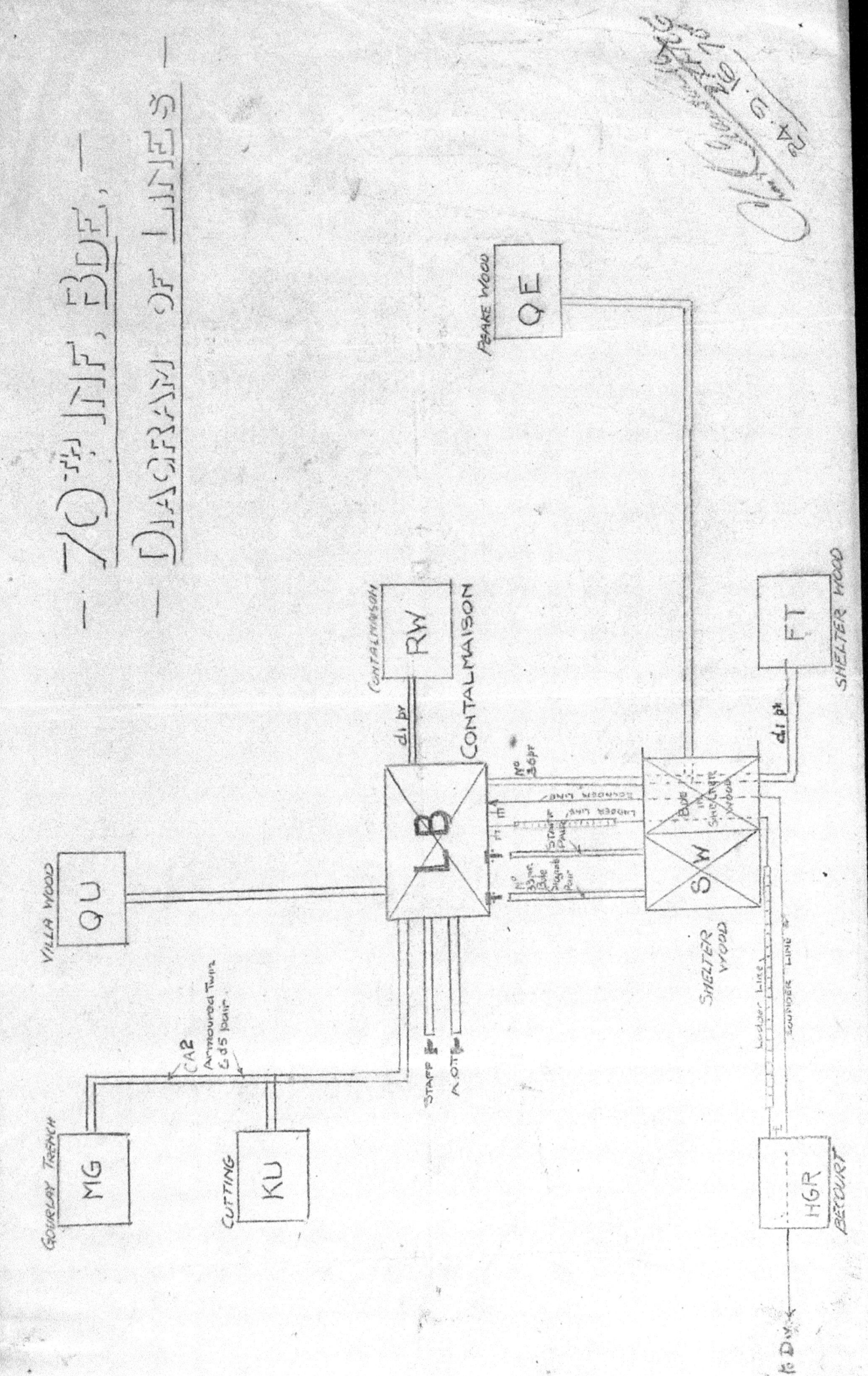

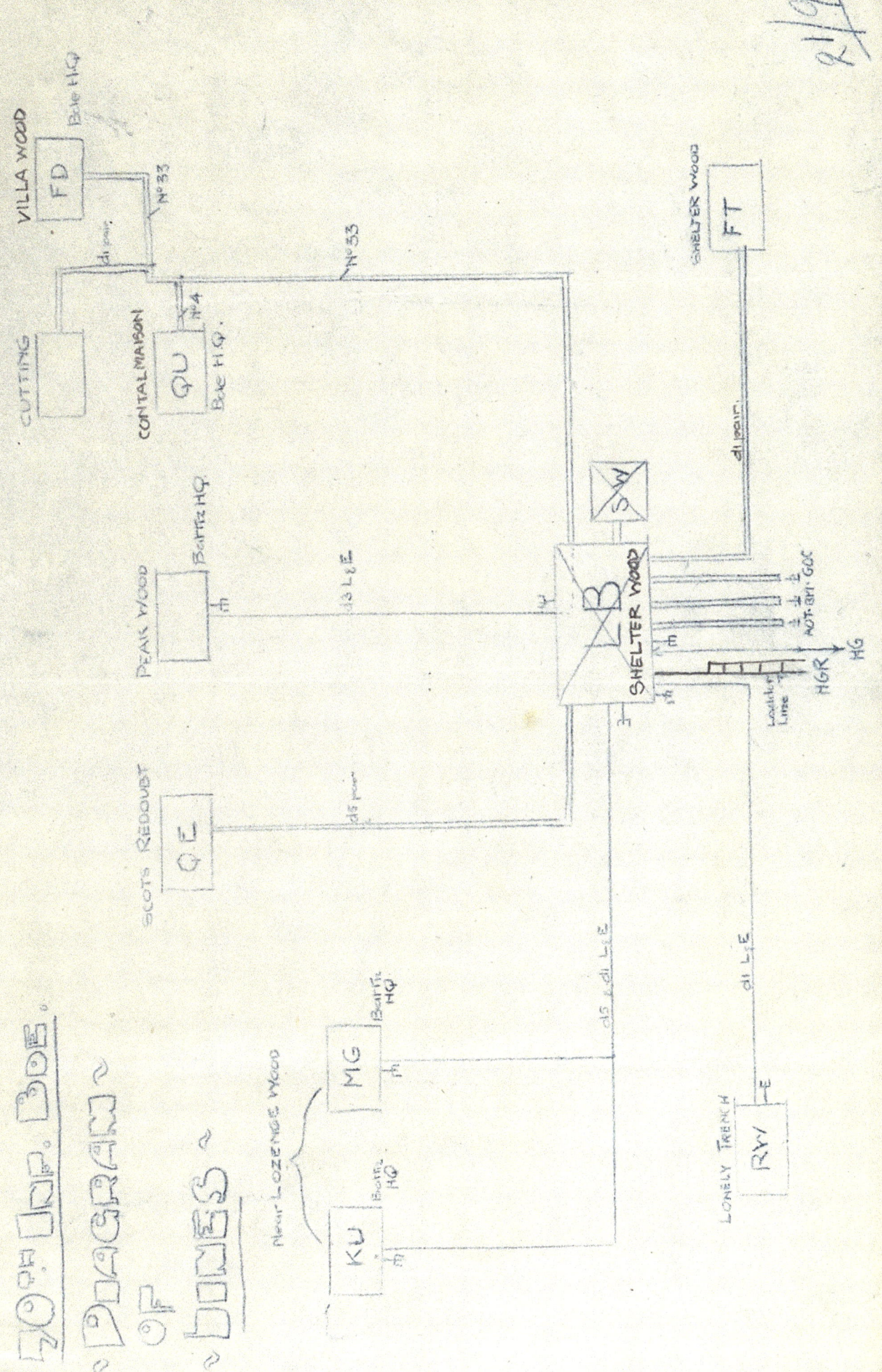

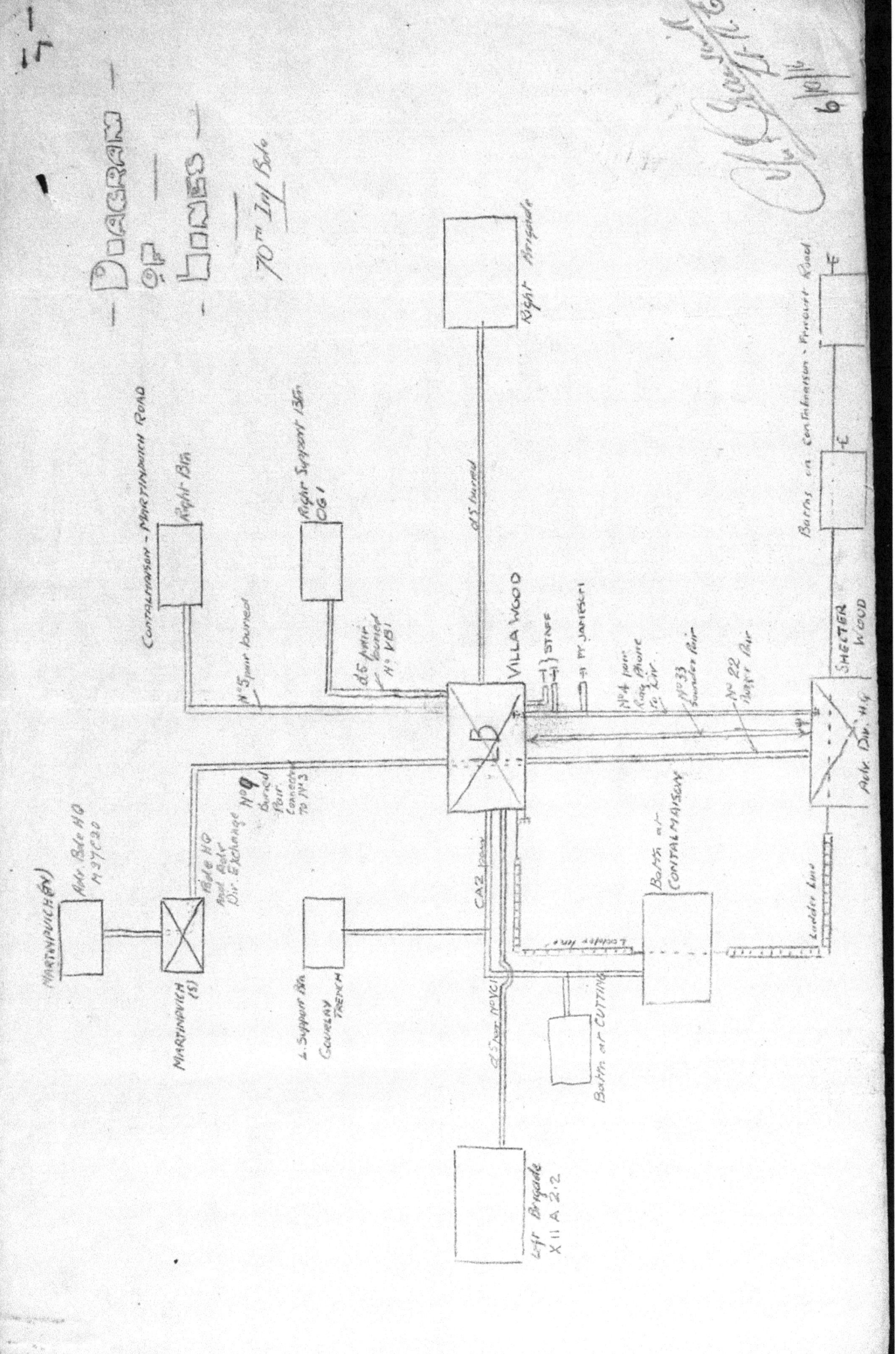

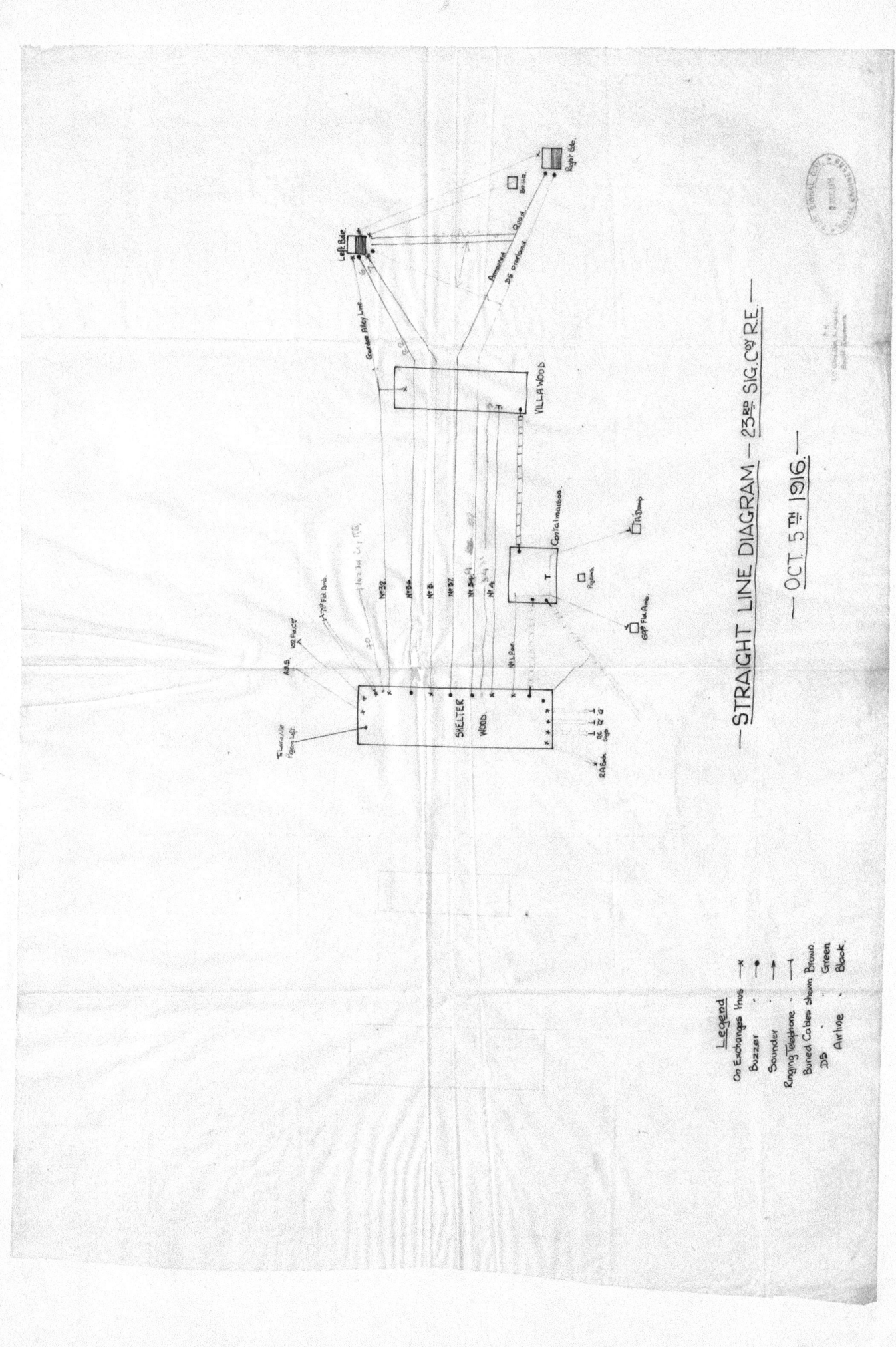

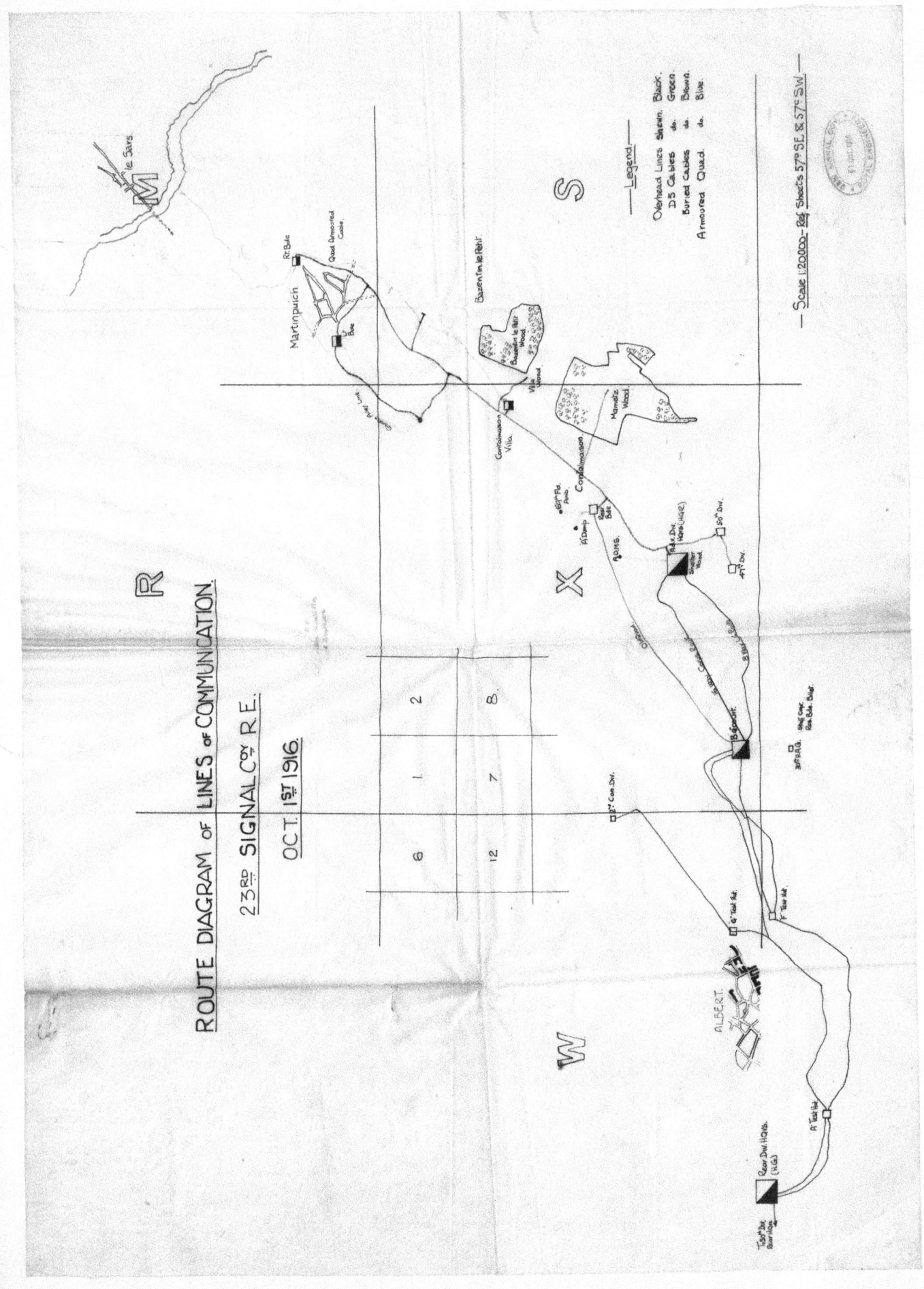

Army Form C. 2118.

Vol 11

WAR DIARY
or
INTELLIGENCE SUMMARY.
(Erase heading not required.)

WAR DIARY
OF
23rd SIGNAL COY R.E.
1st – 31st October 1916.

[signature]
Capt. R.E.
31/10/16

WAR DIARY
or
INTELLIGENCE SUMMARY.
(Erase heading not required.)

Army Form C. 2118.

Place	Date	Hour	Summary of Events and Information	Remarks and references to Appendices
SHELTER WOOD	1/10/16	NOON	Office closed W. of ALBERT & reopened at SHELTER WOOD on advanced Hd qrs. 1 Brigade moved to N.E. end of MARTINPUICH; observed enlarge gun at S.W. end of MARTINPUICH, and however put out at intervals to maintain line. 70th Bde. attacked FLERS line & captured it with small casualties; communication kept up throughout the attack in spite of very heavy shelling.	
"	2/10/16		Work on lines round MARTINPUICH, & a third line run to North end. Improving communications near MARTINPUICH.	
"	3/10/16		Improving communications & laying new line to 2 brigade Hdqrs. in MARTINPUICH.	
"	4/10/16		Improving lines & buries at N. end of MARTINPUICH.	
"	5/10/16		Maintenance & improvement of lines.	
"	6/10/16		68th & 69th brigades attacked and captured LE SARS. Communication maintained throughout in spite of heavy shelling.	
"	7/10/16		Maintenance & improving of lines.	
MONTIGNY	8/10/16	9 AM	Office closed at SHELTER WOOD & reopened at MONTIGNY. Whole of company retained & proceeded to camp at latter place.	
"	9/10/16		1 detachment under Cpl. Bandeau reported to Lt. PRITCHARD at ST GRATIEN.	
"	10/10/16		Company under 2/Lt JAMESON marched to near AMIENS on route for AILLY LE HAUT CLOCHER.	
"	11/10/16			

WAR DIARY
or
INTELLIGENCE SUMMARY.
(Erase heading not required.)

Army Form C. 2118.

Place	Date	Hour	Summary of Events and Information	Remarks and references to Appendices
AILLY-LE-HAUT-CLOCHER	12.10.16	9 A.M.	Office closed at MONTIGNY, reported at AILLY-LE-HAUT-CLOCHER as D.R. office, Company completed move to latter place.	
ST RIQUIER	13.10.16	9:20 A.M.	Office closed & reported at ST RIQUIER at same hour. Resting. CAPT. TILLARD proceeded to RENINGHELST to look at new area.	
"	14.10.16		Advanced party by road in E.L. lorry to RENINGHELST. Company marched to CONTAYVILLE & bivouacked there preparatory to entraining.	
MONTEVILLE	15.10.16			
BUSSEBOOM	16.10.16		Company detrained at 3 A.M., & delivered at BUSSEBOOM at 10 A.M. Office opened at BUSSEBOOM. A house portion and to commence taking over from 2nd Aust. Div. Resting.	
"	17.10.16		Resting.	
"	18.10.16		Advance portion out to 2nd Aust. Division to ——— taking over Report Centre office & test points.	
RENINGHELST	19.10.16			
"	20.10.16	9.0 A.M.	Office closed at BUSSEBOOM, reopened at RENINGHELST at same hour. Company marched to latter place.	
"	21.10.16		Maintenance of lines, & work on completing new signal office. Work in forward area, & continuing of new buried alternative route from Blks. to Bottom.	
"	22.10.16			
"	23.10.16		Improving & maintenance of communications.	
"	24.10.16		Company birthday. G.O.C. inspected at 1 p.m. followed by dinner. Cinema show & concert in evening. Company to duty.	

2nd LT BIDDULPH
Journal the company
A.D.S.S./Forms/C. 2118.

Army Form C. 2118.

WAR DIARY
or
INTELLIGENCE SUMMARY.
(Erase heading not required.)

Instructions regarding War Diaries and Intelligence Summaries are contained in F. S. Regs., Part II and the Staff Manual respectively. Title pages will be prepared in manuscript.

Place	Date	Hour	Summary of Events and Information	Remarks and references to Appendices
RENINGHELST	25.10.16		Work on renewal in forward areas, and on R.A. lines, and buried system.	*see*
"	26.10.16		Signalling class of 5 per battalion commenced at Divnl. Hdqrs. Line built to Train o 70th Inf. School.	*see*
"	27.10.16		Work on forward lines o buried system.	*see*
"	28.10.16		do.	*see*
"	29.10.16		do.	*see*
"	30.10.16		do. 2nd LT. PHILLIP reported for duty.	*see*
"	31.10.16		do.	

Army Form C. 2118.

WAR DIARY
or
INTELLIGENCE SUMMARY.
(Erase heading not required.)

Vol 12

CONFIDENTIAL

WAR DIARY

OF

23rd SIGNAL COY R.E.

1st – 30th November 1916

30/11/16

O.C. 23rd Signal Coy. R.E.

WAR DIARY
INTELLIGENCE SUMMARY
(Erase heading not required.)

Army Form C. 2118.

Place	Date	Hour	Summary of Events and Information	Remarks and references to Appendices
RENINGHELST	1/11/16		Operating and maintenance. Worked on hedging up front line trenches north of here. Linesmen instruction in hut work	
"	2/11/16		Operating and maintenance. Work on horse standings	
"	3/11/16		No 45538 Sergt. Robins R.C. & No 45375 Cpl Hurst E.T. awarded Military Medal.	
"	4/11/16		Operating and maintenance. Work on Lavey tunnel. Steel ore railway track is cutting through the huts. Three died of burial pit.	
"	5/11/16		Operating and maintenance. New burial class formed. Men at 'C' in wooded	
"	6/11/16		Operating and maintenance	
"	7/11/16		Operating and maintenance. Work especially on burial lines in forward area.	
"	8/11/16		Work on connecting up headquarters and RA at report centre	
"	9/11/16		Sent some men to Army Signal School for training	
"	10/11/16		Military Medals awarded to Sappers W.H. G., Shr. A.H. Ward, Lt. Ribson C.E., Maclaren F.H. Adams S.G., Gnr. H.I. Fernie T., Lambert J.A.	
"	11/11/16		41 NCOs and men sent to Army Signal School for training. Work on buried lines at YPRES	
"	12/11/16		Work as above continued. Medal ribbon worn by the General.	

Army Form C. 2118.

WAR DIARY
or
INTELLIGENCE SUMMARY.
(Erase heading not required.)

Instructions regarding War Diaries and Intelligence Summaries are contained in F. S. Regs., Part II and the Staff Manual respectively. Title pages will be prepared in manuscript.

Place	Date	Hour	Summary of Events and Information	Remarks and references to Appendices
RENINGHEST	13/11/16		Finished new work at YPRES	
"	14/11/16		Work on Test Boxes and Faults on Forward Buzzer System.	
"	15/11/16		Opening and maintenance.	
"	16/11/16		2 new ringing systems were installed in RA Bde Batteries and all buzzing instruments removed. Lines from Infantry Bdes and Bns HdQrs into ringing lines and buzzer between Bns also away work.	
"	17/11/16		Installing as on 17th	
"	18/11/16		Operating and maintenance. New buzzer lines formed at Div. HdQrs.	
"	19/11/16		Opening and maintenance.	
"	20/11/16		Opening and maintenance. Work on forward buzzer system.	
"	21/11/16		Operating and maintenance.	
"	22/11/16		Operating and maintenance. Railways took again cut across on line leading to divisional front.	
"	23/11/16		Operating and maintenance. Lots thro' in trench phone circuit started	
"	24/11/16		Operating and	

WAR DIARY
or
INTELLIGENCE SUMMARY

(Erase heading not required.)

Army Form C. 2118.

Place	Date	Hour	Summary of Events and Information	Remarks and references to Appendices
RENINGHELST	25/11/16	—	Shooting and maintenance	—
	26/11/16	—	Shooting and maintenance especially on forward buried lines	—
	27/11/16	—	Work on clearing hot lines improving buried lines and clearing trenches	—
	28/11/16	—	Work on joining up with buried sys. line of Bn. 9 left	—
	29/11/16	—	Work continued as above	—
	30/11/16	—	Shooting and maintenance and general work in tidying up trenches and clearing cables	—

Army Form C. 2118.

Vol 13

WAR DIARY
or
INTELLIGENCE SUMMARY.

CONFIDENTIAL

WAR DIARY

OF

23RD SIGNAL COY., R.E.,

1ST – 31ST DECEMBER 1916

3/1/16

Capt R.E.
O.C. 23rd Signal Coy, R.E.

Army Form C. 2118.

WAR DIARY
or
INTELLIGENCE SUMMARY.
(Erase heading not required.)

Instructions regarding War Diaries and Intelligence Summaries are contained in F. S. Regs., Part II. and the Staff Manual respectively. Title pages will be prepared in manuscript.

Place	Date	Hour	Summary of Events and Information	Remarks and references to Appendices
RENINGHELST	1/12/16		Operating and Maintenance	159
	2/12/16		" " "	169
	3/12/16		" " "	279
	4/12/16		" " "	2A
	5/12/16		" " "	189
	6/12/16		" " "	5B
	7/12/16		" " "	18
	8/12/16		" " "	146
	9/12/16		" Bn. Signallers sent to Army HQ. Schools for further training.	155 188
	10/12/16		"	13
	11/12/16		" W/L Maintenance R.E. joined Coy.	155
	12/12/16		"	
	13/12/16		"	63
	14/12/16		" Started building pole & cable to YPRES as main arm of lines now getting bad.	165
	15/12/16		" Laid air' from Salient. Poles again laid line to YPRES further thin.	18
	16/12/16		" Continued work on poled cable	
	18/12/16		" " " " "	167
	19/12/16		" " " " "	159
	20/12/16		" Continued work on poled cable.	61

2353 Wt. W35141/1454 700,000 5/15 D. D. & L. A.D.S.S./Form/C. 2118.

Army Form C. 2118.

Instructions regarding War Diaries and Intelligence
Summaries are contained in F. S. Regs., Part II
and the Staff Manual respectively. Title pages
will be prepared in manuscript.

WAR DIARY
or
INTELLIGENCE SUMMARY.
(Erase heading not required.)

Place	Date	Hour	Summary of Events and Information	Remarks and references to Appendices
	21.12.16		Clearing and Maintenance built line to Bn. M.G. Coy.	48
	22.12.16		" " " " working party on improving buried lines and poled cable.	48
	23.12.16		" " " " work on poled cable and buried lines.	48
	24.12.16		" " " " " " " "	
	25.12.16		" " " " No out-door work. Bgy. Xmas Dinner	
	26.12.16		" " " " work on poled cable and buried lines. Stations shipped 6'0" [...]	
	27.12.16		From Dewy House to Rud Kui House.	
	28.12.16		Clearing and Maintenance Continued Buried lines 100 September working party.	
			— ditto —	
	29.12.16		Clearing and Maintenance Continued poled cable and buried lines [...] poled cable to YPRES back damaged [...]	
	30.12.16		" " " " Continued work as above. New poled cable to 8th Corp [...]	
			" " " " Stations to VLAMERTINGHE from [...]	
	31.12.16		" " " " to distribution huts [...] continuing all work as above.	

Vol/4

CONFIDENTIAL

WAR DIARY
OF
23RD SIGNAL COY RE

1st — 31st JANUARY 1917

WAR DIARY
or
INTELLIGENCE SUMMARY.
(Erase heading not required.)

Army Form C. 2118.

Place	Date	Hour	Summary of Events and Information	Remarks and references to Appendices
Ravinghem	1-1-17	Operating and Maintenance	Continued work on the prose cable route to VLAMERTINGHE from E.11. 2nd Lt WEBB, 2nd Lieut GO to Salvage from 27½. 2nd Lt GRUBB reports for duty	
	2-1-17	"	Continued burial lines and test depart: from DORMY H° & RUDKIN H°.	
	3-1-17	"	Work as above. Sent signalling party back by II Corps Cavalry establishing stations in forward area.	
	4-1-17	"	"	
	5-1-17	"	Completed metal cable & Continued work on burial lines —	
	6-1-17	"	Work on burial cable	
	7-1-17	"	Completed burial route to Redline. Made stations from Dormy Vance. Two Infantry signal Class commenced. Brigade relief. To burial cable.	
	8-1-17	"	"	
	9-1-17	"	Continued work to O.P.S.	
	10-1-17	"	Completed lines to O.P.S. Commenced burial work from I 21.16.4.4 to I 27.45.4. (75 hum.)	
	11-1-17	"	Continued burial work as above. Artillery Signalling Class commenced 2/Lt Rogers reports for duty. Buried work as above.	
	12-1-17	"	All visual stations established, anomalous work to the final Corps Cavalry party returned to this unit	
	13-1-17	"	to burial cable. 2nd Lt Groth to 2nd Army for course of instruction —	
	14-1-17	"	Continued burial work —	
	15-1-17	"	Visit Argus and Puffin. No F.M. completed by Inventing Cy. Stores all the bus. A.D.S.S./P.M.M./C.2118/ to Redline route completed —	

Army Form C. 2118.

WAR DIARY
or
INTELLIGENCE SUMMARY.
(Erase heading not required.)

Instructions regarding War Diaries and Intelligence Summaries are contained in F. S. Regs., Part II. and the Staff Manual respectively. Title pages will be prepared in manuscript.

Place	Date	Hour	Summary of Events and Information	Remarks and references to Appendices
Ploegsteert	16.1.17		Strength and Maintenance. Company employed stitch bent from YPRES to I.21.b.09. to build cable way & Bde relief — work as above.	MR
	17.1.17		" " " "	MR
	18.1.17		Syd as above. Continued burial cable 100 km	MR
	19.1.17		Completed stitch line — to burial cable.	MR
	20.1.17		Continued burial cable. 100 km	MR
	21.1.17		" " "	MR
	22.1.17		" " "	MR
	23.1.17		to burial cable.	MR
	24.1.17		Buried cable 100 km	MR
	25.1.17		Transferring lines into new dug out at T.16.a.5.8.	MR
	26.1.17		All buried cable work inspected until it rains — work as above.	MR
	27.1.17		Completed work at T.16.a.5.8.	MR
	28.1.17		" "	MR
	29.1.17		Survey poles on RR route to new railway line from hut Plugstt.	MR
	30.1.17		" "	MR
	31.1.17		" "	MR

2353 Wt. W3544/1454 700,000 5/15 D. D. & L. A.D.S.S./Form/C. 2118.

Vol/5

CONFIDENTIAL
WAR DIARY
OF
23RD DIV. SIGNAL COY RE

1st TO 28TH FEBRUARY 1917.

J. Singleton Capt. R.E.
for
O.C. 23rd Div. Signal Coy.
Royal Engineers.

Army Form C. 2118.

WAR DIARY
or
INTELLIGENCE SUMMARY.
(Erase heading not required.)

Instructions regarding War Diaries and Intelligence Summaries are contained in F. S. Regs., Part II. and the Staff Manual respectively. Title pages will be prepared in manuscript.

Place	Date	Hour	Summary of Events and Information	Remarks and references to Appendices
Busseghen	1.2.17		Operating and Maintenance. Continued moving gates to R.K. lines to close new railway track.	
"	2.2.17		Work on R.K. yard as above. Commenced work on lines "K" and "M" dist. trees at I.24.d.04. and I.24.d.23. respectively. Work as above. Laying twin down turnouts from R.Y.15 "M" via "X"	
"	3.2.17		"	
"	4.2.17		"	
"	5.2.17		"	
"	6.2.17		New "K" and "M" lines completed. Also R.Y. 15d lines [?].	
"	7.2.17		Buddlev Alto completed. and H.R. and G.H. lines [?]. Work as above. Commenced turnout lines from Q.15d line at I.24.d.63.7. "O" N. last line at I.24.d.74. Work as above.	
"	8.2.17		"	
"	9.2.17		"	
"	10.2.17		"	
"	11.2.17		"Q" 16 "N" lines completed.	
"	12.2.17		"R.K." yard completed.	
"	13.2.17		Continued laying 20 prs from "D" line through Zillebele Halt of I.22.b.3.of. Work as above. Transferring all this from Rd "E" list line to new "E".	
"	14.2.17		Capt G.E.Grey transferred to 17th Div Signal G.B.G. Capt. F. Nicholson reports for duty as 2nd Command.	
"	15.2.17		Work as above. Commenced work on "E.V.- Z.T.- Z.L" list lines.	

2353 Wt. W2544/1454 700,000 5/15 D. D. & L. A.D.S.S./Form/C. 2118.

WAR DIARY
or
INTELLIGENCE SUMMARY.
(Erase heading not required.)

Army Form C. 2118.

Place	Date	Hour	Summary of Events and Information	Remarks and references to Appendices
Rumylest	16.2.17	—	Training and manoeuvres. Brok as about	
"	17.2.17	—	" " " "	
"	18.2.17	—	" " " "	
"	19.2.17	—	" " " Reconnoitred horse cable hub ring before departed. French field wire	
"	20.2.17	—	" " Took horses & get necessary supple. French field wire and work. Took as above, and a limited train from Q161 Pm 6'20". at 1+4+6+4. (O.P Linge). Took as above "8"15 I.C. completed.	
"	21.2.17	—	" " EV – ZT – ZL tel. legraph completed. Bus RA legraph wires extended.	
"	22.2.17	—	" " Bobs and RA telephone system changed to conform with new establishment. (G.RO 2137)	
"	23.2.17	—	" " Ran open telephone + recharge lines to E Corps	
"	24.2.17	—	" " Company marched to Arneures Capelle	
Arneures Capelle	25.2.17	—	" " Handed over to 59th Div. Bn-signal + S" Coys–Company	
Crayns	26.2.17	—	" " marched to Crayns. Bn. HQ at H. Quen. Established communication with Coys, Bdes, etc Corps, L signals permanent ratio	
"	27.2.17	—	" " Took to Filch, transport lines lanes etc.	
"	28.2.17	—	" " Div. Signal school reopened. Training of signal Coy commenced. Lieut HCJ Pimble R17 refund from II army school.	

Vol 16

CONFIDENTIAL

WAR DIARY

OF

23RD DIV. SIGNAL COY RE

1ST to 31ST MARCH 1917.

[Stamp: 23RD SIGNAL COY. 4 APR. 1917 ROYAL ENGINEERS]

L. Fitzjohn Capt. R.M.F.
R.E.
O.C. 23rd Div. Signal Coy.
Royal Engineers.

Army Form C. 2118.

WAR DIARY
INTELLIGENCE SUMMARY.
(Erase heading not required.)

Instructions regarding War Diaries and Intelligence Summaries are contained in F.S. Regs., Part II. and the Staff Manual respectively. Title pages will be prepared in manuscript.

Place	Date	Hour	Summary of Events and Information	Remarks and references to Appendices
ARQUES	1.3.17	—	Operating and maintenance. Party working with "L" Signal Coy on local routes. Overhauling cable wagon and stores.	I.M.
"	2.3.17	—	Training. Riding, driving & foot drill. Checking stores & instruments.	I.M.
"	3.3.17	—	Work as above.	I.M.
"	4.3.17	—	Work as above.	I.M.
"	5.3.17	—	" " " Detachments practise cable work.	I.M.
"	6.3.17	—	" " " "	I.M.
"	7.3.17	—	Training, drill as above. Detachments practise cable work.	I.M.
"	"	—	Lecture by A.D. Signals VIIIth Corps on "Communications in Mobile Warfare".	I.M.
"	8.3.17	—	Work. Training drill as above. Detachments foot cable work.	I.M.
"	9.3.17	—	Work as above. Lecture.	I.M.
"	10.3.17	—	Company Sports in afternoon, preliminaries.	I.M.
"	11.3.17	—	Inspection. Church Parade.	I.M.
"	12.3.17	—	Overhauling and testing cable wagons.	I.M.
"	13.3.17	—	Riding, driving & foot drill. Detachments foot cable. Lecture.	I.M.

WAR DIARY
or
INTELLIGENCE SUMMARY.
(Erase heading not required.)

Army Form C. 2118.

Instructions regarding War Diaries and Intelligence Summaries are contained in F. S. Regs., Part II. and the Staff Manual respectively. Title pages will be prepared in manuscript.

Place	Date	Hour	Summary of Events and Information	Remarks and references to Appendices
			Continued	
ARQUES	14.3.17	—	Operating and maintenance. Cleaning Wagons. Company sports in afternoon	I.S.
"	15.3.17	—	" " Training: drill as above. Detachments practise field cable	I.S.
"	16.3.17	—	" " Work as above. Slight cable.	I.S.
"	17.3.17	—	" " "	I.S.
"	18.3.17	—	" " Cleaning up billets.	I.S.
"	19.3.17	—	" " Loading up. Advanced party to ESQUELBECQ	I.S.
ESQUELBECQ	20.3.17	—	" " Company marched to ESQUELBECQ. Div. HQ. same place. Established communication with Corps, Bdes etc through Second Army routes.	I.S.
"	21.3.17	—	" " Work on billets. Transport, horse lines etc.	I.S.
"	22.3.17	—	" " Training: drills. Detachments: field cable Visual Signalling. Lieut. C.T. Bravender R.E. transferred to 5th Div Signals. Epretin " " Signalling	I.S.
"	23.3.17	—	" " Work as above	I.S.
"	24.3.17	—	" " " Telegraph work constructed 10.55 am to 11.1 pm to 32 HQ Div orders nr. "	I.S.
"	25.3.17	—	" " Synchronize in Summer Time. Overhauling etc Visual Signalling Training.	I.S.

Army Form C. 2118.

WAR DIARY
INTELLIGENCE SUMMARY.
(Erase heading not required.)

Instructions regarding War Diaries and Intelligence Summaries are contained in F. S. Regs., Part II. and the Staff Manual respectively. Title pages will be prepared in manuscript.

Place	Date	Hour	Summary of Events and Information	Remarks and references to Appendices
			Continued	
ESQUELBECQ	26.3.17	—	Operating and maintenance. Training; drills as above. Visual Practice.	I.S.
"	27.3.17	—	" " " Work as above.	I.S.
"	28.3.17	—	" " " Lieut N.B. Chisholm R.E. joined Corps. and Lieut A.R. Allershand R.E. Transferred to Second Army Signal Coy R.E.	I.S.
"	29.3.17	—	" " " Work as above.	I.S.
"	30.3.17	—	" " " " "	I.S.
"	31.3.17	—	" " " Inspection. Church Parade. Cleaning wagons. Visual practice.	I.S.

Vol 17

CONFIDENTIAL

WAR DIARY

OF

23rd DIV. SIGNAL COY RE

1st to 30th APRIL 1917

J Stephilm Caplain
R.E.
O.C. 23rd Div. Signal Coy.
Royal Engineers.

Army Form C. 2118.

WAR DIARY
or
INTELLIGENCE SUMMARY.
(Erase heading not required.)

Instructions regarding War Diaries and Intelligence Summaries are contained in F. S. Regs., Part II. and the Staff Manual respectively. Title pages will be prepared in manuscript.

Place	Date	Hour	Summary of Events and Information	Remarks and references to Appendices
ESQUELBECQ	1.4.17	—	Operating & Maintenance. Coy. Training in Cable work, drill etc. Signalling Class visual work.	1.Q.
"	2.4.17	—	" Work as above and visual practice	1.Q.
"	3.4.17	—	" "	1.Q.
"	4.4.17	—	" "	1.Q.
"	5.4.17	—	" Signalling Class Test.	1.Q.
"	6.4.17	—	" Signalling Class Inspected.	1.Q.
"	7.4.17	—	" Loading wagons & cleaning up.	1.Q.
BUSSEBOOM	8.4.17	—	Company marched to BUSSEBOOM. Div. H.Q. same place. Took over communications from 39th Div. & 47th Div. in our area.	1.Q.
"	"	—	Signal office closed ESQUELBECQ and opened BUSSEBOOM at 12 noon.	1.Q.
"	9.4.17	—	Operating & Maintenance. Commenced construction of 4 pair trestle route from H.Q. to junction of R.B. and H.K. corps main routes. G.16.c.2.5 to G.29.a.2.5. habitted B.G. route.	2.Q.
"	10.4.17	—	Operating & Maintenance. Changing exchange at E.N.1 & M. Construction as above continued.	1.Q.
"	11.4.17	—	" Construction as above continued.	1.Q.
"	12.4.17	—	" Ran cearie pair to D.A.D.O.S. m Corps P.R. poles.	1.Q.
			Commenced burying route 16 pairs 1.28.d.3.8 to I.29.a.3.7 with Spur 32 pairs to I.29.c.1.8. Rigging party 150 men.	1.Q.

T2134. Wt. W708—776. 500000. 4/15. Sir J. C. & S.

WAR DIARY
or
INTELLIGENCE SUMMARY.
(Erase heading not required.)

Army Form C. 2118.

Place	Date	Hour	Summary of Events and Information	Remarks and references to Appendices
BUSSEBOOM	13.4.17	—	Guarding & maintenance. Addition of 2 pairs to B.S. tents commenced. Came pair to DADOS as above complete.	A.94.
"	14.4.17	—	Burying as above continued.	A.94.
"	15.4.17	—	Work continued on B.S. tents. Sandbagging crossings on new buried route as above.	A.94.
"	16.4.17	—	Sandbagging on new route being as above.	A.94.
"	17.4.17	—	" " "	A.98.
"	18.4.17	—	Continued work of burying as above. Partly 100 men. Took over Q.M. & E.N.I.	A.98.
"	19.4.17	—	" " " " " "	A.92.
"	20.4.17	—	" " " " " "	A.94.
"	21.4.17	—	" " " " " "	A.98.
"	22.4.17	—	" " " " " "	A.98.
"	23.4.17	—	" " " " " " Putting in front beam & hutting	A.98.
"	"	—	Got front on new buried route at junction of Spurs, & beams in to R. & L.	A.94.
"	24.4.17	—	Guarding + maintenance. Continued work of burying as above. Partly 100 men. Touring & beams in.	A.93.
"	25.4.17	—	Lieut A.B. GLOVER R.E. reported for duty with Coy from Fifth Army & taken on strength of Coy.	A.98.

Army Form C. 2118.

WAR DIARY
or
INTELLIGENCE SUMMARY.
(Erase heading not required.)

Instructions regarding War Diaries and Intelligence Summaries are contained in F.S. Regs., Part II. and the Staff Manual respectively. Title pages will be prepared in manuscript.

Place	Date	Hour	Summary of Events and Information	Remarks and references to Appendices
BUSSEBOOM	26.9.17	—	Operating & maintenance. Continued work of burying as above. Trenching & testing in new route.	A.H.
"	27.9.17	—	" "	Construction of — 1.H.
				1.H.
				2.H.
"	28.9.17	—	Came pair to B.T.O. Operating & maintenance. " " Jointing test racks in new house route.	1.H.
			Completed B.T.O. pair.	1.H.
"	29.9.17	—	Operating & maintenance. " "	1.H.
"	30.9.17	—	" " Completed burying of new route as above.	

CONFIDENTIAL

Vol 18

WAR DIARY

OF

23rd SIGNAL COY RE

1st to 31st MAY 1917

J. Elizabeth Cpl/D.M.F.
R.E.
for O.C. 23rd Div. Signal Coy.
Royal Engineers.

WAR DIARY
or
INTELLIGENCE SUMMARY.
(Erase heading not required.)

Army Form C. 2118.

Instructions regarding War Diaries and Intelligence Summaries are contained in F. S. Regs., Part II. and the Staff Manual respectively. Title pages will be prepared in manuscript.

Place	Date	Hour	Summary of Events and Information	Remarks and references to Appendices
BUSSEBOOM	1.5.17		Operating & Maintenance. Advance party to WINNEZEELE.	J.K.
WINNEZEELE	2.5.17		Coy. march to WINNEZEELE. Communication established to Bdes. on X Corps System.	J.K.
"	3.5.17		Operating & Maintenance. Work on present lines. Checking stores.	J.K.
"	4.5.17		" — Coy. training — Cable work & visual in connection with Bde. scheme.	J.K.
"	5.5.17		" — Coy. training — Cable work & visual practice. Overhauling cable wagons.	J.K.
"	6.5.17		" "	J.K.
"	7.5.17		" Coy. training — Cable work & visual in connection with Bde. scheme.	J.K.
"	8.5.17		" "	J.K.
"	9.5.17		" — Cable & visual. Foot & riding drill.	J.K.
"	10.5.17		" "	J.K.
"	11.5.17		" Advance party to BUSSEBOOM & bivouacs to forward position.	J.K.
BUSSEBOOM	12.5.17		Coy. march to BUSSEBOOM. Taking over from 19th DIVN. Communication established to Bdes.	J.K.
"	13.5.17		Operating & Maintenance. Commenced work on buried cable route from I.28 d.28 to I.27 c.5.9 and I.21 d.3.6	J.K.
"	14/5/17		party of 500 men.	J.K.
"	14.5.17		" " party of 200 men.	J.K.
"	15.5.17		" Work on buried cable route continued as above.	J.K.

T2134. Wt. W708—776. 500000. 4/15. Sir J. C. & S.

Army Form C. 2118.

WAR DIARY
or
INTELLIGENCE SUMMARY.
(Erase heading not required.)

Instructions regarding War Diaries and Intelligence Summaries are contained in F. S. Regs., Part II. and the Staff Manual respectively. Title pages will be prepared in manuscript.

Place	Date	Hour	Summary of Events and Information	Remarks and references to Appendices
BUSSEBOOM	16.5.17.		Operating + Maintenance. Work on buried cable route I 27 c 5.9 to I 26 a 7.1. Building in and fitting up test boxes	J.W.
"	17.		party of 200 men.	J.W.
"	17.5.17.		Work as above.	J.W.
"	18.5.17.		" " "	J.W.
"	19.5.17.		" " "	J.W.
"	20.5.17.		" " "	J.W.
"	21.5.17.		Work on ditches Cable & Shallow trenches E.N.I.16 H.15 c. Commenced work on buried cable route I.21 C 75.80 to I. 21 d 25.65. 20 fins. party of 100 men fitting	J.W.
"			up test boxes & racks.	J.W.
"	22.5.17.		Work as above.	J.W.
"	23.5.17.		" " "	J.W.
"	24.5.17.		" " "	J.W.
"	25.5.17.		Heading in and fitting up test boxes & racks. Banking trench 1 platoon	J.W.
"	26.5.17.		" "	J.W.
"	27.5.17.		" "	J.W.
"	28.5.17.		" "	J.W.

T2134. Wt. W708-776. 500090. 4/16. Sir J. C. & S.

Army Form C. 2118.

WAR DIARY
or
INTELLIGENCE SUMMARY.
(Erase heading not required.)

Instructions regarding War Diaries and Intelligence Summaries are contained in F. S. Regs., Part II. and the Staff Manual respectively. Title pages will be prepared in manuscript.

Place	Date	Hour	Summary of Events and Information	Remarks and references to Appendices
BUSSEBOOM	29.5.17		Gunnery + trailtrainers. Bathing roster - 1 Platoon.	J.S.
"	30.5.17		" " " "	J.S.
"	31.5.17		" " " "	J.S.

T2134. Wt. W708—776. 500000. 4/15. Sir J. C. & S.

Vol 1

CONFIDENTIAL
WAR DIARY
OF
23RD SIGNAL COY RE
1st to 30th JUNE 1917

F. Stapleton
Capt. R.M.F
for O.C. 23rd Div. Signal Coy.
Royal Engineers.

Army Form C. 2118.

WAR DIARY
or
INTELLIGENCE SUMMARY.
(Erase heading not required.)

Instructions regarding War Diaries and Intelligence Summaries are contained in F. S. Regs., Part II. and the Staff Manual respectively. Title pages will be prepared in manuscript.

*[Stamp: 286␣ SIGNAL COY. * 5 JUL 1917 * ROYAL ENGINEERS]*

Place	Date	Hour	Summary of Events and Information	Remarks and references to Appendices
BUSSEBOOM	1.6.17		Operating & maintenance. Digging shallow trenches H.15.c.6 H.22.a.15 & laying 3 7/air cables. Working party 200. Repairing HC-II route. Working party 1/Platoon.	I.M.
"	2.6.17		" Jointing 7/air cables as above.	I.M.
"	3.6.17		" As above. Leading in to R.E. Office at H.22.a.	I.M.
"	4.6.17		" As above.	I.M.
"	5.6.17		" Wiring Office at H.22.a.	I.M.
"	6.6.17		" R.E. Opened at H.22.a.15.	I.M.
"	7.6.17		"	I.M.
"	8.6.17		"	I.M.
"	9.6.17		"	I.M.
"	10.6.17		"	I.M.
"	11.6.17		"	I.M.
"	12.6.17		Company marched to BERTHEN. Established communication all Bdes. through 9th + 10th Corps system.	I.M.
BERTHEN	13.6.17		Operating & maintenance. Work on lines + billets.	I.M.
"	14.6.17		"	I.M.
"	15.6.17		" Overhauling wagons & stores.	I.M.

WAR DIARY
INTELLIGENCE SUMMARY.
(Erase heading not required.)

Army Form C. 2118.

Place	Date	Hour	Summary of Events and Information	Remarks and references to Appendices
BERTHEN	16.6.17		Operating & maintenance. Visual established to Brigs.	J.L.
"	17.6.17		" "	J.M.
"	18.6.17		" " Training of company. Foot drill.	J.M.
"	19.6.17		" " As above.	J.M.
"	20.6.17		" " "	J.M.
"	21.6.17		" " "	J.M.
"	22.6.17		" " "	J.M.
"	23.6.17		" " " Arty. Signalling class assembled.	J.M.
"	24.6.17		" " "	J.M.
"	25.6.17		" " "	J.M.
"	26.6.17		" " "	J.M.
"	27.6.17		" " "	J.M.
"	28.6.17		" " "	J.M.
"	29.6.17		" " " heading in and wiring office at ZEVECOTEN.	J.M.
"	30.6.17		Coy marched to MIC-MAC Camp. Office opened at ZEVECOTEN and office taken over from YX at Mic-Mac Camp. Communication established to Bdes & 2 DA.	J.M.

CONFIDENTIAL

WAR DIARY

OF

23rd Div. Signal Coy RE

1st to 31st July 1917

J. Skipton Capt. R.M.F.

for O.C. 23rd Div. Signal Coy.
Royal Engineers.

WAR DIARY
INTELLIGENCE SUMMARY
(Erase heading not required.)

Army Form C. 2118.

Place	Date	Hour	Summary of Events and Information	Remarks and references to Appendices
ZEVECOTEN	1-7-17		Operating maintenance. Work on hardwood Tunnel to I29.d.6.0 Working party 80 men	A.H.
"	2-7-17		" do	A.H.
"	3-7-17		" Jointing Party on new route	A.H.
"	4-7-17		" Cable carried forward for laying route I30b4.65 to I30a9.3 Working party 25 men	A.H.
"	5-7-17		" Digging cable trenches from I30b4.65 to I30a9.3 Working party 75 men	A.H.
"	6-7-17		" "	A.H.
"	7-7-17		" Digging Canada St Working Party 100 men	A.H.
"	8-7-17		" "	A.H.
"	9-7-17		" "	A.H.
"	10-7-17		" Digging from Battn HQ (I29d6.4) forward to I30c3.0 Working party 100 men	A.H.
"	11-7-17		" and digging I29c85 to I29c9.0 150 men	A.H.
"	12-7-17		" Digging from Battn HQ (I29d6.4) forward to I30c30 Working party 150 men	A.H.
"	13-7-17		" " "	A.H.
"	14-7-17		" Finished digging forward of Battn HQrs	A.H.
"	15-7-17		" Leading in cables, lifting test racks on new route. Clearing open trench from C.R. Box to L Box Working party 150 men	A.H.

WAR DIARY
or
INTELLIGENCE SUMMARY.
(Erase heading not required.)

Army Form C. 2118.

Instructions regarding War Diaries and Intelligence Summaries are contained in F.S. Regs., Part II. and the Staff Manual respectively. Title pages will be prepared in manuscript.

Place	Date	Hour	Summary of Events and Information	Remarks and references to Appendices
ZEVECOTEN	16.7.17		Operating and maintenance. Clearing from Trench from CR Box to L Box. Working party 100 men	J.H.
"	17.7.17		" Replacing 7 pair by armoured cable from MICMAC to FC2 Box.	J.H.
"	18.7.17		" Digging Shallow Trench LCR to B.HQ (East) Working Party 50 men	J.H.
"	19.7.17		" and constructing 4 pair H4 pole route from H 26 a.9.6 to H 21 d 8.3	J.H.
"	20.7.17		As above "	J.H.
"	21.7.17		As above "	J.H.
"	22.7.17		As above. Micmac Signal Office handed over to 2nd Division.	J.H.
METEREN	23.7.17		Company marched to METEREN. Signal Office established at Meteren Mairie.	J.H.
"	24.7.17		Work on horse lines & billets. Infantry Instrument Class commenced.	J.H.
"	25.7.17		Visual practice & station work for Signallers. Cable Wagon Practice.	J.H.
"	26.7.17		Instrument Class. As above	J.H.
"	27.7.17		Instrument Class. Visual work to Bleu - station Practice. Lecture on Cable jointing & linemen duties.	J.H.

Army Form C. 2118.

WAR DIARY
or
INTELLIGENCE SUMMARY.
(Erase heading not required.)

Instructions regarding War Diaries and Intelligence Summaries are contained in F. S. Regs., Part II. and the Staff Manual respectively. Title pages will be prepared in manuscript.

Place	Date	Hour	Summary of Events and Information	Remarks and references to Appendices
METEREN	28.7.17		Operating & maintenance Instrument Class. Football. Lecture on DIII Division 'phone. Visual Test. Lecture to linesmen on their duties.	A.H. A.H.
"	29.7.17		" Instrument Class. Cable jointing class. Visual class Test with buzzer lamp	A.H. A.H.
"	30.7.17		" " Cablewagon practice - laying cable. Visual class on harp reading	A.H. A.H.
"	31.7.17		" Instrument Class. Cable wagon practice - laying cable. Visual Class on practice stations. Lt A.B. Glover 2/6 (TF) Transferred to "I" Corps Signal Coy.	A.H. 221

CONFIDENTIAL

WAR DIARY

OF

23RD DIV SIGNAL COY RE

1ST to 31ST AUGUST 1917

WAR DIARY
INTELLIGENCE SUMMARY
(Erase heading not required.)

Army Form C. 2118.

Instructions regarding War Diaries and Intelligence Summaries are contained in F.S. Regs., Part II. and the Staff Manual respectively. Title pages will be prepared in manuscript.

Place	Date	Hour	Summary of Events and Information	Remarks and references to Appendices
METEREN	1-8-17		Operating & Maintenance. Instrument Class. Foot drill. Cable jointing for Linemen. Visual practice.	
"	2-8-17		" Instrument Class. Instruction in Linemen duties. Visual practice.	
"	3-8-17		" Examination of Instrument Class. Visual established between METEREN and MERRIS. Cable jointing instruction for Linemen.	
"	4-8-17		" Cable jointing instruction for Linemen. Departure of Instrument Class to WIZERNES.	
"	5-8-17		" Church Service. Advance party to WIZERNES. Work on cable wagons & tables.	
"	6-8-17		" Company march to WIZERNES.	
WIZERNES	7-8-17		" Communication established to Bde & Coys. Work on wagon lines.	
"	8-8-17		" As above.	
"	9-8-17		" Company march to EPERLECQUES.	
EPERLECQUES	10-8-17		" Work on wagon lines. Cable jointing for Linemen. Visual scheme.	
"	11-8-17		" Bde. Visual established to Bde. Slow cable practice for new linemen.	
"	12-8-17		" Church Service. Work on Cable wagons. Visual to Bde.	
"	13-8-17		" Cable Wagon Practice. Visual to Bde. Lecture on Map Reading. Gas drill.	
"	14-8-17		" Visual to Bde. Foot Drill. Gas Drill. Cable jointing practice.	

Army Form C. 2118.

WAR DIARY
INTELLIGENCE SUMMARY.
(Erase heading not required.)

Instructions regarding War Diaries and Intelligence Summaries are contained in F.S. Regs., Part II. and the Staff Manual respectively. Title pages will be prepared in manuscript.

Place	Date	Hour	Summary of Events and Information	Remarks and references to Appendices
EPERLECQUES	15-8-17	Operating + Maintenance	Cable Wagon Practice. Visual and Wireless lectures in Bell Scheme. Gas Drill.	
"	16.8.17	"	Cable Wagon Practice. Lecture on Map Reading. Visual + Map Reading Scheme.	
"	17-8-17	"	Gas drill. Cable Wagon instruction for new entrants. Foot drill. Gas drill.	
"	18-8-17	"	Cable Wagon Practice. Flagdrill, Semaphore. Cable jointing + Mapreading lecture. Lt R. W. Rogoff posted to this unit from 2nd Army Signals.	
"	19.8.17	"	N.F. Church Service. Flag drill. Map Reading + lumumis telethie.	
"	20.8.17	"	Semaphore. Mapreading. Visual Scheme. Buried Station Practice.	
"	21.8.17	"	As above.	
"	22.8.17	"	As above.	
"	23.8.17	"	Coy march to NOORDEPEENE. Adv. party to RENINGHELST.	
NOORDEPEENE	24.8.17	"	Coy march to RENINGHELST.	
RENINGHELST	25.8.17	"	Take over from 14th Div. Signals.	
"	26.8.17	"	As above. Coy march to DICKEBUSCH.	
DICKEBUSCH	27.8.17	"	ii Lieut A.G. Colsten R.E. joined unit from 3rd Div. Signals Co R.E.	
"	28.8.17	"	Installing wireless set amplifier and power supplies.	
"	29.8.17	"	Patrolling, repairing of cover Routing routes through or	
"	30.8.17	"	S. side. Laying overhead lines.	
"	31.8.17	"	Burying cable 14 pairs from H1 Box to Halfway House.	

Vol 22

CONFIDENTIAL

WAR DIARY

OF

23rd SIGNAL COY RE

1ST TO 30th SEPT. 1917.

N.B. Chisholm.
Lt. RE
for OC 23rd Signal Co RE

Army Form C. 2118.

WAR DIARY
or
INTELLIGENCE SUMMARY.
(Erase heading not required.)

Instructions regarding War Diaries and Intelligence Summaries are contained in F. S. Regs., Part II. and the Staff Manual respectively. Title pages will be prepared in manuscript.

Place	Date	Hour	Summary of Events and Information	Remarks and references to Appendices
Dickebusch	1-9-17		Operating and maintenance. Bringing cable H.I. to HALFWAY HOUSE.	MSC
"	2-9-17		" Company marched to Steenvoorde. Hand over to 24th Division.	MSC
Steenvoorde	3-9-17		" Cleaning wagons and harness.	MSC
"	4-9-17		" Company march to Lederzeele.	MSC
Lederzeele	5-9-17		" Cleaning wagons and harness.	MSC
"	6-9-17		" Exercise horses. Linesmen class. Jointing and testing.	MSC
"	7-9-17		" "	MSC
"	8-9-17		" "	MSC
"	9-9-17		" Church Parade. Inspection of iron rations and gas helmets.	MSC
"	10-9-17		" Bathing Parade. Anti gas instruction by Div: Gas Officer.	MSC
"	11-9-17		" "	MSC
"	12-9-17		" Advance party sent to Burgomark Farm. Dickebusch.	MSC
"	13-9-17		" Company march to Steenvoorde.	MSC
Steenvoorde	14-9-17		" Take over from 24th Division.	MSC
Burgomark	15-9-17		" Testing lines. Cleaning wagon & harness.	MSC
"	16-9-17		" Church Parade. Bringing to Advanced Brigade HQ.	MSC

Army Form C. 2118.

WAR DIARY
or
INTELLIGENCE SUMMARY.
(Erase heading not required.)

Instructions regarding War Diaries and Intelligence Summaries are contained in F.S. Regs., Part II. and the Staff Manual respectively. Title pages will be prepared in manuscript.

Place	Date	Hour	Summary of Events and Information	Remarks and references to Appendices
Burgomaster	17-9-17		Operating and Maintenance. Bringing cable to Advanced Brigade HQ.	MSC
"	18-9-17		" Testing out pairs on the new 100 pair bary	MSC
"	19-9-17		" as above	MSC
"	20-9-17		" Bottle.	MSC
"	21-9-17		" 33rd Div. Sigs. officers shown over lines.	MSC
"	22-9-17		" Party went to Torr Top to pick up new circuits on 100 pr. bway.	MSC
"	23-9-17		" as above.	MSC
"	24-9-17		" 33rd Div Sig. linesmen shown over routes.	MSC
"	25-9-17		" Company march to Westoutre. 23rd Div: hand over to 33rd DIV.	MSC
West Outre	26-9-17		" Cleaning wagons & harness.	MSC
"	27-9-17		" as above	MSC
"	28-9-17		" Company march to Burgomaster Farm. Dickebusch. Take over from 33rd Div.	MSC
Burgomaster	29-9-17		" Testing lines. Cleaning wagons and harness	MSC
"	30-9-17		" Overhead route broken by tanks. Lines test through temporarily with cable.	MSC

Vol 23

CONFIDENTIAL

WAR DIARY
OF
23RD SIGNAL COY RE
1st to 31st October 1917.

A Affleck Captain RE
for O.C. 23rd Div. Signal Coy.
Royal Engineers.

WAR DIARY

INTELLIGENCE SUMMARY.
(Erase heading not required.)

Army Form C. 2118.

Instructions regarding War Diaries and Intelligence Summaries are contained in F. S. Regs., Part II. and the Staff Manual respectively. Title pages will be prepared in manuscript.

Place	Date	Hour	Summary of Events and Information	Remarks and references to Appendices
Burgomaster Tn Dickebusch	1-10-17		Operating tramaintenance. Load Wagons. clean up camp.	I.S.S.
Berthen	2-10-17	"	Company march to Berthen. Handed over to 5th Div.	I.S.S.
"	3-10-17	"	Work on wagons & camp	I.S.S.
"	4-10-17	"	"	I.S.S.
"	5-10-17	"	Infantry Signalling Class Commences (52 men)	I.S.S.
"	6-10-17	"	Infantry Signalling class. Gas drill. W. Pre Gray NF admitted to Hospital	I.S.S.
"	7-10-17	"	"	I.S.S.
"	8-10-17	"	Signalling class. Riding Drill. Foot Drill	I.S.S.
"	9-10-17	"	do. Gas Drill	I.S.S.
Chateau Segard	11-10-17	"	Company march to Chateau Segard and take over from 7th Div.	I.S.S.
"		"	Work on overland lines from R.C. & H.H. (I,?,C4?) to Stope Croton Groom	I.S.S.
"		"	Gratin to H.O. continue field route from Gunners lodge to H.O.	I.S.S.
"	12-10-17	"	Work as above & constructing pole cablehut route & pair to connect with Corps route at "J" 30.c (I?b.a.6?)	I.S.S.
"	13-10-17	"	Ditto	I.S.S.
"	14-10-17	"	Ditto	I.S.S.
"	15-10-17	"	Ditto. Infantry class sent to X Corps School	I.S.S.

Army Form C. 2118.

WAR DIARY
INTELLIGENCE SUMMARY.
(Erase heading not required.)

Instructions regarding War Diaries and Intelligence Summaries are contained in F. S. Regs., Part II. and the Staff Manual respectively. Title pages will be prepared in manuscript.

Place	Date	Hour	Summary of Events and Information	Remarks and references to Appendices
Chateau Segard	16.10.17	Operating & maintenance	Competing work. Lt R.W.GRAY NF transferred to base Depot (P.B)	A.A.
"	17.10.17	"	do.	A.A.
"	18.10.17	"	do.	A.A.
"	19.10.17	"	do.	A.A.
"	20.10.17	"	do.	A.A.
"	21.10.17	"	Work Completed	A.A.
"	22.10.17	"	Advance Party move to Wizernes	A.A.
EECKE	23.10.17	"	Company march to EECKE	A.A.
WIZERNES	24.10.17	"	Company march to Wizernes. Birthday of formation of Company.	A.A.
"	25.10.17	"	Work on horse lines & billets	A.A.
"	26.10.17	"	Cleaning Wagons, harness	A.A.
"	27.10.17	"	Limewash Class	A.A.
"	28.10.17	"	As above	A.A.
"	29.10.17	"	As above. Birthday of company celebrated by Dinner & outing.	A.A.
"	30.10.17	"	As above. Lieut A.Watt R.S.F joined unit from 2nd Army.	A.A.
"	31.10.17	"	As above	A.A.